Table of Contents

W9-BRV-465

Dedication

Our first book was dedicated to my daughter Sherri, who died of melanoma cancer in February 1983. The course of my life changed at that time which led me to meeting my husband Marvin. We were married in 1987.

This second book is dedicated to Marvin's younger son Ben. He was diagnosed with multiple sclerosis in September 1994. Ben's courage during this period of his life is very inspiring.

We also want to include Marvin's oldest son Steve and my son Rich in this dedication. We are very proud of all three of our sons, and they are all three collectors. Ben and Steve are both avid marble collectors. Steve has one of the nicest collections of marbles we have ever seen. Rich likes sports, so he collects baseball cards. Of course, we encourage their interest in wall pockets and they all look for wall pockets for us.

Correspondence

If you would like to correspond with Joy and Marvin Gibson concerning wall pockets, they may be contacted at:

P.O. Box 217
Ozark, MO 65721

Pricing Information

The values in this book should only be used as a guide. They are not intended to set prices which vary due to local demand, condition and availability. Auction and dealer prices also vary greatly. Neither the authors nor the publisher assume responsibility for any losses that might be incurred as a result of consulting this guide.

COLLECTORS GUIDE TO

WALL POCKETS

Affordable, Unique & Other$
Book II

by
Joy and Marvin Gibson

Photography & Artwork
by
Marvin Gibson

© 1997
Joy and Marvin Gibson

L-W Book Sales
P.O. Box 69
Gas City, Indiana 46933

ISBN #: 0-89538-088-9

Published by: L-W Book Sales
               P.O. Box 69
               Gas City, IN 46933

Please write for our free catalog.

COVER DESIGN BY

JOY AND MARVIN GIBSON

Front Cover Information

All the wall pockets on the front cover are shown and priced inside the
book except for the large red one Joy is holding at the bottom of the page.
According to the dealer/owner, this is a rare Sumida Gawa wall pocket
with applied monkeys. These pockets were being made in Japan in the late
1800's up to 1970. Our wall pocket dates back mid to late 1800's and is
priced at $1000 to $1500.

Acknowledgments

We wish to thank all the wonderful people who have worked with us to make this book possible. Without each of you we could not have finished it. First on our long list is, of course, L-W Books, who took a chance on our first book and are willing to trust us one more time. They are really great to work with. Thank you so much.

Many people shared their wall pocket collections with us, either by letting us come into their homes to take pictures or sending us pictures and the information we needed to write this book. We certainly enjoyed meeting those of you who invited us into your homes, cementing the friendships we had started through the mail and phone calls. Those of you who have taken the time to take photos and send them to us, we hope to meet you one day soon. There is no way we can thank you enough or give you the credit you all deserve, but we want you to know we truly appreciate each of you.

Lana and Kenneth Moore, Springfield, MO (Joy's sister); Rob and Carolyn Milbourn, Hastings, MI; Harry and Phyllis Jordan, Pittsburg, KS; Virginia and Jim Walker, Hannibal MO; Frank and Kathleen Holt, Columbia, MO (Noritake); Bobbie and Alan Bryson, Tuckahoe, NY (Glass); Linda D. and Allen White, Lapeer, MI; Jack Hooper, Springfield, MO; John and Karen Cerilli, Scottsdale, AZ; Fred Dodson, Lockhart, TX; Opal Hampton, Dundas, IL; Viola of Akron, OH; Laura Brubeck, Unionville, VA (McCoy); Fred and Sarah Wolfe, (U.S. Air Force) Panama (McCoy); Craig Nissen, WI (McCoy); Kathy Morgan, Oklahoma City, OK; Wanda Coulter, Springfield, MO; Penny Williams, Linn Creek, MO; Tom and Linda Burnett, Nixa, MO; Red and Mary Ann Huston, Fidelity, MO; Bobbie and Sandra Farris, Bertrand, MO; Mike Montalvo, Nutley, NJ; Ruth Ann Nida, Spencer, WV; Kay Sheetz, Enumclaw, WA; Carol Davis, Plato, MO; Jackie Huey, Antelope, CA; Alan and Barbara Wilson, Huntington Beach, CA; George and Carol Ethel (Kaleidoscope Antiques), Dallas, TX; Paul and Rosemary Dodds (Antique Corner), West Plains, MO; Historic Mercantile Mall, Tontitown, AR; Doberts Antique Mall, Rogers, AR; Scott Nelson, Sante Fe, NM (Van Briggle); Pat Warner, Oklahoma City, OK (Frankoma); Steve and Jane Mueske, (GrandTiques) Cohasset, MN ; D.F. and Grace Vanlandingham, (Van-tiques) Belton, MO; Freda Dyer, Wichita, KS (Tiara exclusives); Burdell and Doris Hall, Morton, IL (Authors of Morton's Potteries - 99 Years); Ralph and Terry Kovel, Beachwood, OH (Authors - Kovel's books on Marks and Antiques and Collectibles); Carol Bess White, Portland, OR (Author - Made in Japan); Jeffrey, Sherrie and Barry Hershone, Lake Mary, FL (Authors - Peters and Reed); and last, but certainly not least, Joretta and John Donald, Springfield, MO, for the use of the office at Pack-N-Stack to take pictures and write this book.

We certainly hope we have not left anyone out, as we have tried to keep a record of all who have been a part of the work on this book and appreciate each of you. It has been a long project, so if you helped in any way and do not see your name here, please forgive us, we thank you very much. God bless you all.

Introduction

Wall pocket collecting has become a way of life for us since we began in 1987. Our collection started with one we got in a box at an auction by chance and grew in intensity– we now have over four thousand.

We spent a lot of time looking for information about our wall pockets. We didn't find much until after we wrote our first book, then wall pocket collectors and dealers who bought wall pockets only for resale started writing to us and sharing their knowledge. Together we have all learned a lot over the past two years and we certainly appreciate all that you have taught us. As our knowledge grows, our love of wall pockets also grows.

Wall pockets began in the Victorian era, when the ladies of the home made pockets out of cloth, lace, yarn, cardboard, wood and anything else they had on hand. These they hung on the wall to store paper, pens, combs, gloves, scarves and the many other items they wanted to hide from the sight of visitors. The more affluent the household, the more elaborate the wall pockets were.

The wall pockets we find the most were made from the late 1800's until the present time, the most favored being the ones made in the late 1800's into the 1950's and by American potteries or glass factories. Many foreign countries like Germany, Japan, England and Czechoslovakia are well known for making many beautiful and unique wall pockets.

Most potteries and glass factories seem to have made some wall pockets, yet many did not mark their pieces, which makes them very difficult to identify. Another reason it is hard to identify a piece is the potters, artists and glass makers moved from one factory to another with irregular frequency, taking their ideas with them, so there are similarities in the clays and glazes at the potteries and in the quality and styles of the glass. There was a lot of copying going on also, not only in the United States. We have found wall pockets marked "Made in Japan" that look just like ones "Made in America"– of course the quality is a lot different. So don't be misled just because it looks like a Weller, look on the back for a mark. If there is not a mark, check the weight and quality. Get to know the product that you buy, buy what you like, then enjoy.

We have found that wall pocket collectors are a very special type of people. Both men and women collect them, some collect only glass, some only Roseville, Weller, McCoy or Birds, etc., but we all seem to have one thing in common. We are obsessed with them. We never have enough and we keep looking for that special one. That is another thing that is special about wall pockets–there are so many different ones, made by so many different countries, that there are some that appeal to each of us.

Unlike our first book on wall pockets, which was made up of our own personal collection (except for 44 wall pockets), this second book includes wall pockets from several different collections, as you can tell from the pictures. We certainly appreciate all the help we have had from our wall pocket friends.

There is one other thing I would like to say to the readers of this book. We are not experts on wall pockets, we are learning just like everyone else. We have researched as many wall pockets as we possibly could by talking to (what we consider) experts in their fields, reading, searching the libraries, and compiling all the information we have received through the mail. We are not sure anyone could be an expert on wall pockets– there are just so many of them. But we will continue to look for more information and hopefully pass it on to you.

How It All Started

My first wall pocket

This cuckoo clock is the first wall pocket we ever bought. In 1987, we were at an auction in Des Moines, Iowa and bought a box of things for a dollar. The wall pocket was in the box. As I had never seen a wall pocket before, Marvin had to tell me what it was called and what it was used for. The tail had been broken off and glued back on carelessly, but it was so cute I hung it on our kitchen wall. After that I started seeing them everywhere and buying the ones I liked. We are still buying them after 9 years and love each one as much as the first one.

Cuckoo clock with yellow bird and green leaves, the time is set at "4 o'clock", and has two pine cone pendulums hanging from brass chains, marked with a red paper label with gold markings "LEFTON'S REG. U.S. PAT. OFF. EXCLUSIVES JAPAN".   **$25 - 30**

The market value on this wall pocket with the tail broken and repaired is only $5.00"?", but as the sentimental value to me is beyond money, it can not be bought for any amount.

The last wall pocket for Book II

This is the last wall pocket we "put together" for this book. The last part of May 1996, we were in a remote flea market in the southwest corner of Missouri and found the lid and bottom to this Fenton Lavabo. Imagine our surprise when we went into another flea market (at least 100 miles northeast of the first one) only a few weeks later and finding the piece we needed to complete the set.

Fenton Lavabo, white hobnail milk glass, three piece set, marked with a partial foil Fenton label.
$125 - 175

NOTE:
Unless otherwise stated in the description, the size of the wall pockets in this book can be determined by the number of holes in the pegboard. There is 1 inch between each hole.

CALIFORNIA POTTERIES

The state of California has never received the recognition it deserves for it's pottery industry – especially the wall pockets that were made there. As you can see in this chapter, there were many very beautiful and unique wall pockets made in California.

ROW 1:

1. Square shape, yellow with green flower, mark incised "Walker - 958".   **$15 - 20**

2. Square shape, mauve with pink flower, mark incised "Walker - 958".   **$15 - 20**

Both of the above were made by Walker Potteries, Monrovia, California, owned by Joseph Walker. Early 1940's until the mid 1950's.

ROW 2:

Oriental girl sitting, pink and black, marked in black ink stamp "WEIL WARE w/BURRO - MADE IN CALIFORNIA" and impressed "4045". Made by California Figurine Co., founded by Max Weil, 1940 until 1955.   **$35 - 40**

ROW 3:

1. Woman figure, aqua blue, trimmed with gold, mark incised "California - Originals #645". Made by Heirlooms of Tomorrow at Torrance and Manhattan Beach, California, 1947 until 1980's. These were usually sold by Montgomery Wards, Penney's, Sears and other large department stores.   **$20 - 25**

2. Man figure, marked and information is the same as above.   **$20 - 25**
                    Price per pair –   **$45 - 60**

The above pair are extra large. The man is 12 inches tall and the woman is 11 inches. Remember, throughout this book you can measure by the holes in the peg board, 1 inch between holes.

California Potteries

ROW 1:

   1. Grapes with leaf, chartreuse color, trimmed   **$15 - 20**
       with gold, mark incised "MADE IN CALIF. #302".

   2. Brown wall pocket with yellow rose, mark incised   **$40 - 50**
       "CALIF - USA". Made by Marsh Industries of Glendale
       and Los Angeles, Calif. 1950-late 1980's.

   3. Strawberry, red trimmed with gold, mark incised   **$15 - 20**
       "MADE IN CALIF. #304".

ROW 2:

   1. Yellow hen with closed eyes, no marks.   **$25 - 30**

   2. Yellow rooster with open eyes, no marks.   **$25 - 30**

     This pair was in our first book on page 212 and unidentified.
     We now have them identified as made by Dan Davis of
     California in 1950. The rooster has the original price on
     the back, "70¢".

ROW 3:

     Rooster, fighting cock, brown color, trimmed with gold,   **$35 - 45**
     mark incised "MADE IN CALIF USA CWP". This is one
     of an opposite pair and comes in several different colors.

NOTES:

In the late 1940's there is reported to have been over 800 potteries in operation at one time in California. Many of them were very small family owned operations set up in a garage or shed and did not last very long, but many of them went on for many years and made a lot of very collectable pieces of pottery.

California Potteries
CALIFORNIA CLEMINSON

ROW 1:

    1. Black Cooking Pot. On the front it reads "the kitchen is   **$20 - 25**
the HEART of the HOME!". Marked on the back is the
Cleminsons seal "THE CALIFORNIA b CLEMINSONS –
HAND-PAINTED©".

    2. Artist Paint Palette, white with fruit and vegetables.   **$35 - 45**
On the front it reads "Cooking is an ART!". Also marked
with green ink stamp on the back is the Cleminsons seal
"THE CALIFORNIA b – CLEMINSONS HAND-PAINTED ©".

ROW 2:

    1. Black teapot. On the front it reads " . . . a penny   **$20 - 25**
SAVED is a penny EARNED". Unmarked, but looks like
a California Cleminson.

    2. Spinning Wheel, brown, on the front it says "Busy   **$40 - 50**
hands make a HAPPY HEART!". Marked with a green
ink stamp on the back is the Cleminson seal that reads
"THE CALIFORNIA b CLEMINSONS HAND- PAINTED ©".

ROW 3:

    1. Red Bells, marked with the Cleminsons seal in black ink   **$35 - 40**
stamp "THE CALIFORNIA b CLEMINSONS HAND-PAINTED ©".

    2. Small straight necked pitcher, mark incised "Calif.".   **$15 - 20**

NOTE:

*George and Betty Cleminson started making pottery in their garage in
Monterey Park, California in 1941 as a hobby. They called it "CLEMINSON
CLAY". It became so popular they had to build a larger facility at El Monte,
California in 1943 and hired about 50 employees. At that time they changed
the name to "THE CALIFORNIA CLEMINSONS". By 1947 they had around
160 employees. In the early 1960's, the cost to keep the original quality
was so great the Cleminsons decided to close the pottery in 1963.*

California Potteries

ROW 1:

    1. Green Trivet with mauve rose, mark, incised "HOLLYWOOD
CERAMICS © – Made in Calif.". The pottery was located in
Los Angeles, Calif. 1948 to 1976.   **$30 - 40**

    2. Chartreuse wall pocket with pink and mauve roses, mark
incised "JOHANNES Brahn Calif. 230 USA". The pottery was
located at Reseda and Los Angeles, California, 1945 - 1956.   **$30 - 35**

ROW 2:

    1. Bamboo pattern wall pocket, brown and green, mark incised
on the back are some oriental figures, marked on the bottom
with brown ink stamp is a grape leaf with "JAENESSTS
CAPISTRANO CALIF. ©".   **$20 - 25**

    2. Green leaf, mark incised "Hazel Hutchins of Calif.".   **$25 - 30**

ROW 3:

    1. Toothbrush Holder, pink and green, marked in black ink stamp
"TULIP TOOTH BRUSH HOLDER © Artist Barn, Fillmore, Calif.
(use nail in each hole)". Has two holes in the back to hang it up
and four holes in front for toothbrushes.   **$40 - 60**

    2. Pink Pot in metal holder, mark incised "MIRAMAR of Calif. ©
1955 - 266". This is made to hang or sit. It has the original
price tag $1.79. Made in Los Angeles, Calif. 1952 - 1960's.   **$20 - 25**

    3. Small tulip match holder, pink and green, marked with a black
ink stamp "TULIP MATCH HOLDER © Artist's Barn, Fillmore,
Calif.". Original price on the back 89¢.   **$30 - 40**

15

California Potteries

ROW 1:

1. Spice Box Wall Pocket, tan color with red house, marked in black ink stamp "POPPYTRAIL BY METLOX - MADE IN CALIFORNIA". This pattern was called Homestead Provincial and it was in the 1950 Company brochure. Catalog number 1482. **$60 - 70**

2. Match Box Holder, tan color with red house, marked in black ink stamp "POPPYTRAIL BY METLOX - MADE IN CALIFORNIA". This pattern was called Homestead Provincial and it was in the 1950 Company brochure. Catalog number 1481. **$60 - 70**

NOTE:

METLOX was founded in 1927 at Manhattan Beach, California. The company went out of business in 1989. The name METLOX came from the metallic oxide that was mined in California and used in the METLOX glazes. Poppytrail became a line the first time in 1934 until 1942, then came out again in 1958. It was popular for a few years and then came back again in 1978.

ROW 2:

1. Western Saddle, green, mark incised "ROYAL DURAN - CALIF.". **$40 - 50**

2. Wall Pocket, grey trimmed with gold, mark incised "Re-go of California © 1952 - #202". **$20 - 25**

ROW 3:

1. Horse Collar, brown, mark incised "ROYAL DURAN – CALIF". **$40 - 50**

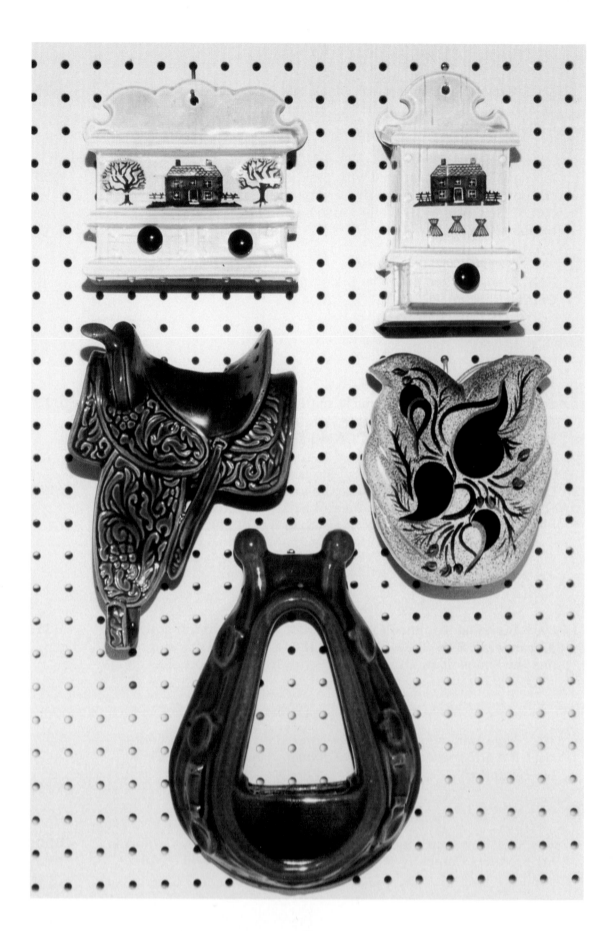

California Potteries

ROW 1:

    1. Dark Grey Fish trimmed with black, not marked. Identified   **$25 - 30**
as made by "Tropic Treasures", Ceramicraft of San Clemente,
California.

    2. Mama Fish, white trimmed with pink, marked in brown ink   **$35 - 40**
stamp "Tropic - Treasures by Ceramicraft, San Clemente,
CALIF. PAT. NO. D-169, 159". Also has a baby fish and gold
bubbles as a set.

    Baby Fish, marked in brown ink stamp "COPYRIGHT ©
Ceramicraft, SAN CLEMENTE, CALIF".

ROW 2:

    1. Yellow Fish trimmed with black, marked in brown ink stamp   **$25 - 30**
"Tropic Treasures © by Ceramicraft - San Clemente, CALIF.
PATENT PENDING – CERAMICRAFT San Clemente, Calif".

    2. Light Pink Fish trimmed in black, marked in brown ink stamp   **$25 - 30**
"Tropic Treasures © by Ceramicraft SAN CLEMENTE, CALIF.
PAT. NO. 169, 519". This piece also has two bubbles.

ROW 3:

    1. Dark Pink Fish trimmed in black, marked in brown ink stamp   **$25 - 30**
"Ceramicraft SAN CLEMENTE, CALIFORNIA". This marking
has the shape of an artist's palette with three paintbrushes.

NOTE:

*The above Mama Fish, Yellow Fish and Light Pink Fish did not
have the artist palette marking, although they were all made
by "Ceramicraft".*

    2. Sea Shell, tan, mark incised "California Arts". Made by California   **$20 - 25**
Art Products Company of Los Angeles, California 1945-1948.

California Potteries

ROW 1:

1. Green square with elf and leaf, no markings, but identified   **$20 - 25**
    by the elf's features and clothes as a "Treasure Craft –
    Pottery Craft" of Compton and South Gate, Calif.

2. Skunk with hand-painted flowers, mark incised "De Lee Art ©".   **$30 - 35**
    De Lee stood for the names of the founders, Delores and Lee
    Mitchell. The pottery was located in Los Angeles, California
    from the late 1930's until the early 1950's.

3. Skunk with hand-painted flowers, mark in black ink stamp   **$20 - 25**
    "8204". This piece was probably made in Japan, and is a
    copycat. Notice the difference in size.

NOTE:

*Both of the above skunks have a hole through their tails. Tied
through this hole was a tag that said, "If your bathroom is
occupied by someone who's a thinker, I hope he burns a match
of mine and makes me a DE-STINKER". These skunks were made
to hang in the bathroom to hold matches.*

ROW 2:

1. Purple Grapes with chartreuse leaves, mark incised "Treasure   **$20 - 25**
    Craft, Compton, California".

2. Purple Grapes with green leaves, not marked, but identified   **$20 - 25**
    as a "Treasure Craft – Pottery Craft" from others we have that
    are marked.

ROW 3:

Brown Pot wall pocket in metal hanger. The pocket is incised   **$15 - 20**
"TREASURE CRAFT 19 © 58 COMPTON CALIF". Treasure
Craft also made cookie jars, canister sets and planters.

Treasure Craft was also known as doing business in the name of
"Pottery Craft". They were in production at Compton and South
Gate, California from 1945 to 1988. In 1988 the company was
purchased by Pfaltzgraff of York, Pennsylvania.

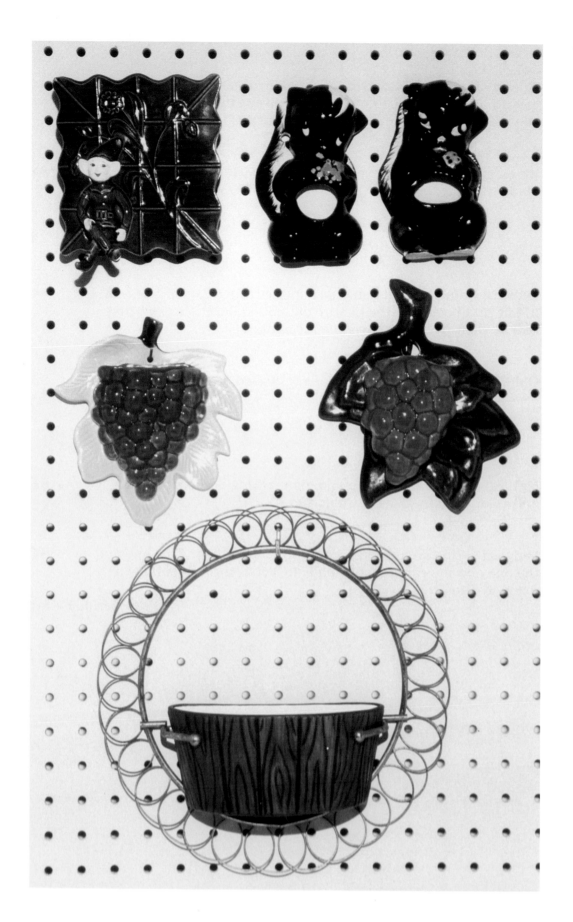

California Potteries

ROW 1:

1. Bunch of Bananas with Red Elf, mark incised "GILNER 19 ©   **$40 - 45**
   50 CALIF". Made by Gilner Pottery, Culver City, California. The
   company was in operation in the 1950's.

2. Elf on green leaf, mark incised "Cali Crown ©". Identified as   **$20 - 25**
   Made in California.

ROW 2:

1. Lady Elf riding a green fish, mark incised "GILNER ©". She was   **$40 - 45**
   in our first book, but the picture did not do her justice, we just
   had to show her again. *Note the fancy dress.*

2. Old Man Elf sitting on a violin, mark incised "California".   **$35 - 40**

ROW 3:

1. Man Elf sitting on a green piano, no markings. It has the style   **$15 - 20**
   and color combinations of California.

2. Lady Elf sitting on a green accordion, no markings. This one and   **$15 - 20**
   the one above were probably made to sell as a set. Identified as
   made in California.

   Price per pair – **$30 - 40**

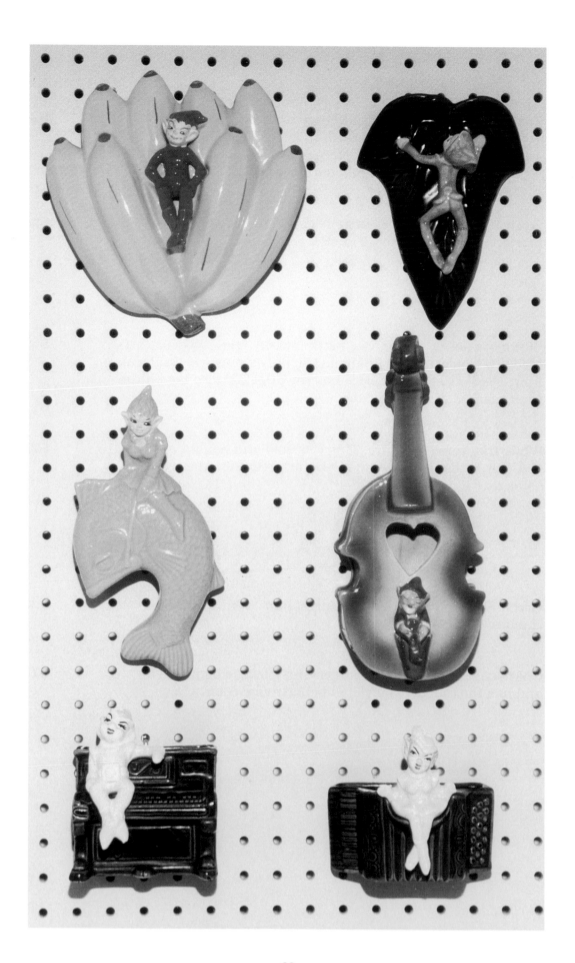

California Potteries

ROW 1:

1. Bear standing by oak leaves with acorns, chartreuse and
   green, the mark is hard to read, (it looks like) "Ca_ _ _".
   This piece is probably California, because it is light weight
   with the California style and chartreuse color.

   $20 - 25

2. Squirrel eating acorn. Chartreuse and green color, no
   markings, but matches #1 in style and color.

   $20 - 25

ROW 2:

1. White Iris flower and leaves, mark incised "Iris California Arts".
   Made by California Art Products Co. of Los Angeles, California
   from 1945 - 1948. This piece has the original price tag on the
   front marked at $5.00 a pair.

   $25 - 30

2. White Iris, same as above. This was sold and bought as part
   of a pair, although they are not a mirrored pair. Marked the
   same as #1.

   $25 - 30

   Price per pair – **$50 - 60**

ROW 3:

1. Green Flowers, mark in black ink stamp "Don Rolen –
   Handmade, California".

   $25 - 30

2. Chartreuse Leaves, no markings. This piece is light weight
   and has the California style and chartreuse color.

   $15 - 20

California Potteries

ROW 1:

1. Violin, white trimmed with pink and blue, marked with a paper label "CALIFORNIA FIGURINE M -CO- W HAND DECORATED". Made by California Figurine Company, Los Angeles, California. Established by Max Weil from 1940 - 1955. Incised on the back "44-ME", probably made in 1944. $25 - 30

2. Salt and Pepper shaker holder, white with yellow and brown stripes, marked with a paper label "Genuine HANDMADE Starnes CALIFORNIA U.S.A.". Made by Walter Starnes Ceramics. This company made "Lava Bo's" (their spelling) and match box holders among other things, but the most interesting piece we have seen is a "cigarette pack dispenser", it holds a carton of cigarettes and hangs on the wall. It has a slot in the side so you can see how many packs are left. These items were made in the 1950's. $15 - 20

ROW 2:

1. Black Teapot with red cherries and chartreuse leaves, no markings, but has the California style and colors. $15 - 20

2. Black Coffee Pot with red cherries, no markings. Same pottery as one above. $15 - 20

ROW 3:

1. Drummer Boy with drum, white trimmed with pink and blue. No markings, but has the style and color combinations of California Pottery. $15 - 20

2. Sword Fish, pink trimmed with gold, marked with a paper label "FREEMAN-McFARLIN – Originals © EL MONTE, CALIF". It also has an artist mark in black "R". $25 - 30

3. Match Box Holder, white with rooster and flowers, marked with part of a paper label that reads "CALIFORNIA". $20 - 25

27

California Potteries

ROW 1:

1. Mammy sitting on an old style yellow iron, mark incised "©".   **$60 - 75**
Identified as "Hollywood Ceramics" by the shape of the Mammy.

2. Black Native in palm tree with an alligator trying to get him. The   **$125 - 150**
mark is in blue ink stamp "MADE IN JAPAN". This piece is on
this page in order to keep all black memorabilia together.

   Will be shown again in the Japan chapter.

ROW 2:

1. Black Chef on yellow flour scoop, mark incised "Hollywood   **$60 - 75**
Ceramics ©".

2. White Chef on yellow flour scoop, mark incised "Hollywood   **$40 - 50**
Ceramics ©".

ROW 3:

1. Black Chef sitting on an old cook stove, chartreuse in color,   **$60 - 75**
mark incised "Hollywood Ceramics ©".

2. Black Chef sitting on an old cook stove, dark green in color,   **$60 - 75**
mark incised "Hollywood Ceramics ©".

NOTE:

*Hollywood Ceramics of Los Angeles, California is a good example
of some of the many potteries that operated in Southern California,
and very little is known about it. They were known to make pottery
for Maddux of California in the late 1940's into the 1950's. We do
know that they made some very high quality wall pockets.*

29

California Potteries

ROW 1:

1. Mammy in green clothes, mark in black ink stamp "5601 B COVENTRY – Made in U.S.A.". Made by Coventry Ware, Inc., Barberton, Ohio from 1932 to 1960's. This piece has a shallow pocket in the head for (scent?, rings?, scouring pads? etc.).

    This piece was placed on the page in order to keep all the black memorabilia together.

    $45 - 55

2. White Chef sitting on a skillet with a fried egg, sunny side up, not marked. Could be California, (it just looks good with all the other chefs).

    $20 - 25

ROW 2:

1. Mammy sitting by an old style yellow washing machine, mark incised "Hollywood Ceramics © Pat Pend.".

    $150 - 175

2. Mammy sitting by an old style chartreuse washing machine, mark incised "Hollywood Ceramics © Pat Pend.".

    $150 - 175

ROW 3:

1. White Chef sitting on a chartreuse match box holder, no markings. Identified as "Hollywood Ceramics" by the color and shape of the chef.

    $40 - 50

2. Black Chef sitting on a chartreuse food grinder, no markings. Identified as "Hollywood Ceramics" by the color and shape of the chef.

    $60 - 75

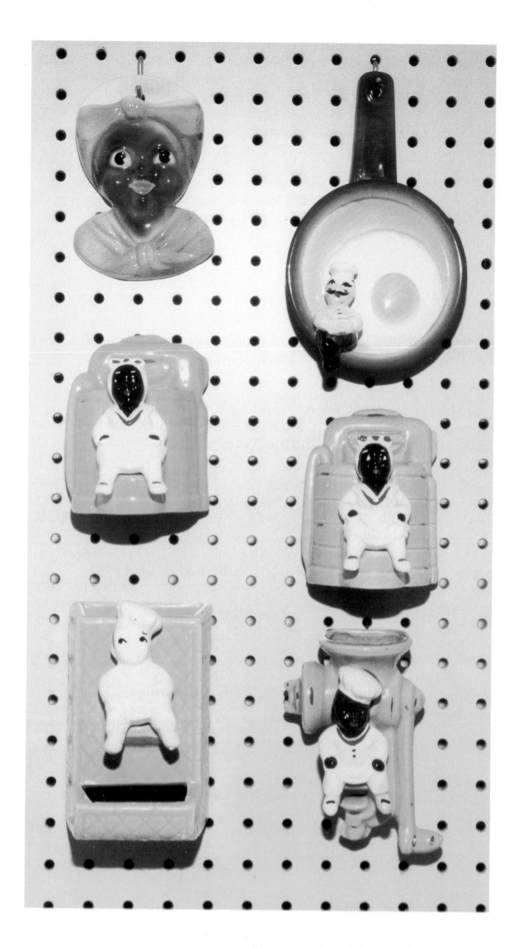

California Potteries

This page contains wall pockets made by Japan and unknown makers. We are including them at the end of the California chapter in order to keep all the black memorabilia together. Some of these wall pockets will be shown again in the Japan miscellaneous chapter.

ROW 1:

1. Black woman with red glass earrings.   **$30 - 35**

2. Black woman with green glass earrings. Both are trimmed   **$30 - 35**
   with gold, marked with a gold foil labels that reads "MADE
   IN JAPAN", and has a black ink stamp that reads "8A170".

   Priced per pair – **$65 - 80**

ROW 2:

1. Black figure dressed in red with gold colored turban, gloves   **$15 - 20**
   and curled toed shoes, made of chalk, 9".

2. Set consists of two black cherubs and a planter, each piece
   is a pocket. The cherubs have a hole in the top of their heads.
   All pieces have gold accents and a impressed mark "JAPAN".

   Cherubs priced each – **$15 - 20**
   Opposite pair of cherubs – **$35 - 45**
   Planter – **$10 - 15**
   Three piece set – **$95 - 125**

3. Same as #1 Black figure, made opposite, both have blue eyes.

   Priced per pair – **$35 - 50**

ROW 3:

Pair of Native Dancers, gold color, 13" tall, mark incised "B 550",
maker unknown.

Priced per pair – **$50 - 75**

Pair of Black heads, man on the left, woman on the right, both
have big gold earrings, both are marked with brown ink stamp
"JAPAN".

Priced each – **$25 - 30**
Priced per pair – **$60 - 70**

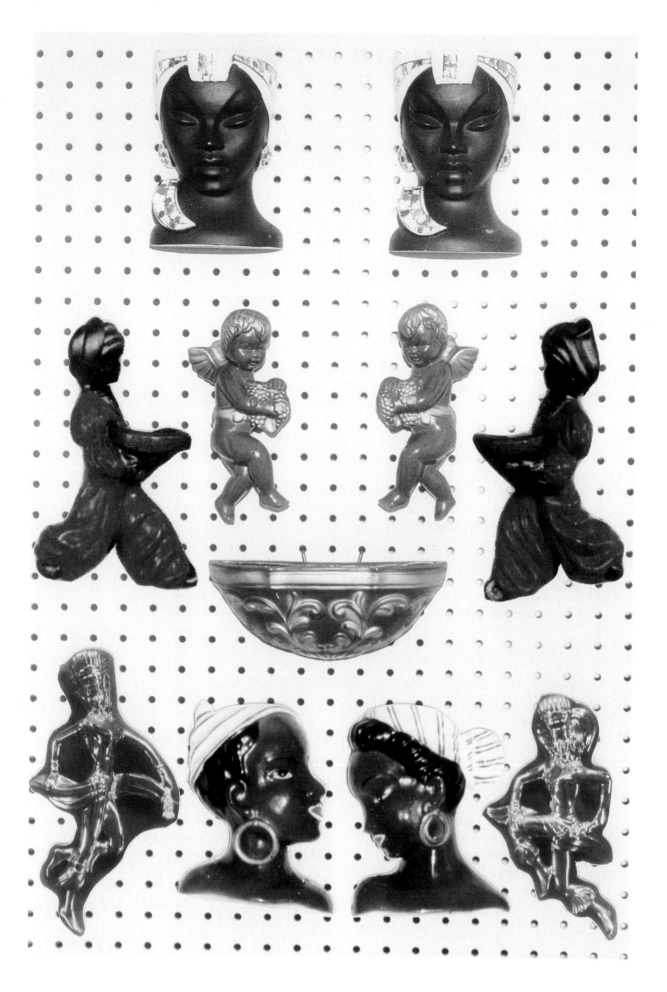

33

CAMARK POTTERY

Camark Pottery was founded in Camden, Arkansas, by Samuel Jacob Carnes in 1926. Over the many years Mr. Carnes owned and operated Camark Pottery, some very well known artists worked for him. The Pottery was sold in 1962 after Mr. Carnes death. The new owners operated it at minimum production over the next twenty years. It closed in 1982.

ROW 1:

1. Torch, aqua blue, mark incised that reads "CAMARK USA N-22".   **$20 - 25**

2. Flour Scoop, yellow with embossed flowers, mark incised   **$20 - 25**
   "USA CAMARK N-45". Original price tag read $3.50.

3. Diaper, green, with an incised mark that reads "837 USA",   **$25 - 30**
   identified as Camark.
   This was mistakenly identified in our first book as McCoy.

ROW 2:

1. Small Cup and Saucer, pink, mark incised "167" on bottom of   **$20 - 25**
   cup. Identified as Camark.

2. Large Cup and Saucer, white with mauve trim, no mark. Identified   **$25 - 30**
   as Camark. The factory catalog number was 150-D, the D stood
   for decorated. This piece was made either right or left handled.

3. Small Cup and Saucer, yellow with multi-color flowers, mark   **$20 - 25**
   incised "167" on bottom of cup. Identified as Camark.

ROW 3:

A group of Cowboy Boots. There are four single boots in colors of white, aqua blue, pink and black. These were all originally sold in pairs and tied together with a leather thong. Camark catalog price was $6.00 per dozen, catalog #565. We bought the dark blue pair as shown (not original cord). The leather thongs are missing on most of these boots and we usually find them as singles.

Price each – **$3 - 5**
Price per pair – **$7 - 12**

CZECHOSLOVAKIA

Czechoslovakia made some of the most beautiful and unique wall pockets in history. The quality is superb. When a person becomes familiar with the style and brilliant colors of Czechoslovakian wall pockets, they are very easy to identify.

ROW 1:

1. Bird with long yellow tail and berries, marked with red ink stamp "10" and "Made in Czechoslovakia", and also impressed "5952 A".   **$50 - 65**

2. Bird with yellow fanned tail, marked with red ink stamp "39" and "Made in Czechoslovakia", and also impressed "5680 B".   **$60 - 80**

3. Bird with long red tail and pine cones, marked with red ink stamp "31" and "Made in Czechoslovakia", and also impressed "5957 A".   **$45 - 60**

ROW 2:

1. Toucan Bird with large yellow beak, marked with red ink stamp "41" and "Made in Czechoslovakia". Original price is on the back "$1.45".   **$55 - 70**

2. White wall pocket with bright multicolored flowers, marked with black ink stamp "CZECHOSLOVAKIA with a dragon", also impressed "961". This wall pocket is in the "Peasant Art Design" which was popular in the early 1900's and is hard to find.   **$65 - 75**

3. Crested Bird, marked with red ink stamp "31" and "Made in Czechoslovakia", and also impressed "5950 B".   **$50 - 60**

Czechoslovakia

ROW 1:

1. Bird on spiral sea shell, white pearl color in lustre, marked with red ink stamp "4" and "Made in Czechoslovakia", and also impressed "2" and "6080".   **$50 - 60**

2. Small grey and pearl lustre ware wall pocket, marked with black ink stamp "TRADEMARK CORONET CZECHOSLOVAKIA REGISTERED" with a wreath and crown seal. The original price is on the back "29¢".   **$25 - 35**

3. Yellow bird with flower and bow on a fan, marked with red ink stamp "45" and "Made in Czechoslovakia", also impressed "12" and "5891 A".   **$50 - 60**

ROW 2:

1. Owl on limb, marked with red ink stamp "18" and "Made in Czechoslovakia", also impressed "6205 A".   **$55 - 65**

2. Green bird on limb, marked with red ink stamp "32" and "Made in Czechoslovakia".   **$50 - 60**

3. Owl on castle, marked with red ink stamp "Made in Czechoslovakia" and also impressed "6082".   **$55 - 65**

ROW 3:

1. Large bird on limb with a nest, marked in red ink stamp "45" and "Made in Czechoslovakia", and also impressed "5675 H".   **$60 - 75**

2. Small bird on limb by nest, marked with a red ink stamp "33" and "Made in Czechoslovakia", and also impressed "5675 A".   **$45 - 55**

NOTE:

Czechoslovakia was known to make different sizes in the same design, as shown above.

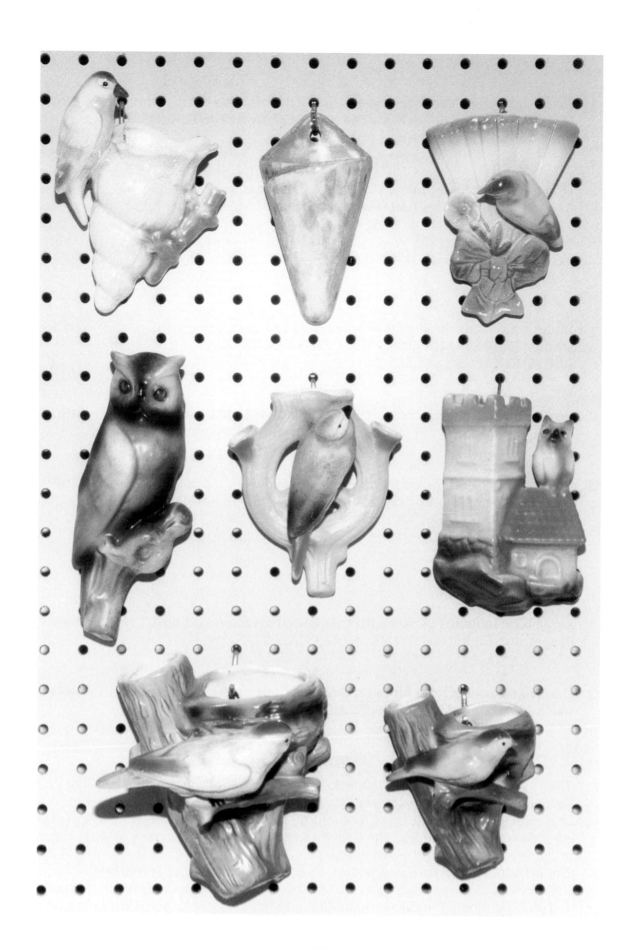

Czechoslovakia

ROW 1:

1. Cone shaped with orange flowers, marked with a black ink stamp "TRADE MARK-CORONET-CZECHOSLOVAKIA-REGISTERED", 7 1/2" tall. **$30 - 40**

2. Woodpecker on limb, marked with a red ink stamp "Made in Czechoslovakia", 7 1/2" tall. *Hand drawn by Marvin Gibson.* **$60 - 75**

3. Information and marked same as #1. **$30 - 40**

ROW 2:

1. White cone shape with yellow flower, marked with a black ink stamp "TRADE MARK-CORONET CZECHOSLOVAKIA-REGISTERED", 5 1/2" tall. **$25 - 30**

2. Bird on pineapple, marked with a red ink stamp "Made in Czechoslovakia", 7" tall. *Hand drawn by Marvin Gibson.* **$60 - 75**

3. Dark grey cone shape with red and yellow flowers, marked with a black ink stamp "CELEBRATE-REGISTERED-MADE IN CZECHOSLOVAKIA", 6 1/2". **$30 - 40**

ROW 3:

1. Large blue majolica pocket with tree limb, blossoms and bird design, mark impressed "CZECHOSLOVAKIA", 7 1/2" tall. **$80 - 90**

2. Green wall pocket with birds on limbs of cherry tree, marked with black ink stamp "MADE IN CZECHOSLOVAKIA", 7" tall. **$60 - 70**

NOTE:

The Czechs and the Slovaks settled in Bohemia hundreds of years ago. On October 28, 1918, they were set free of the Austrian and Hungarian domination and was granted a country of their own. The country was named Czechoslovakia after the two nationalities. The Czechs were very prosperous people with expertise in light engineering and glass making.

The beautiful glassware and pottery that we find today that is marked Czechoslovakia was made after 1918. The country was split again on January 1, 1993, becoming the Czech Republic and the Slovak Republic. But the name Czechoslovakia still continues to be used on some trade marks.

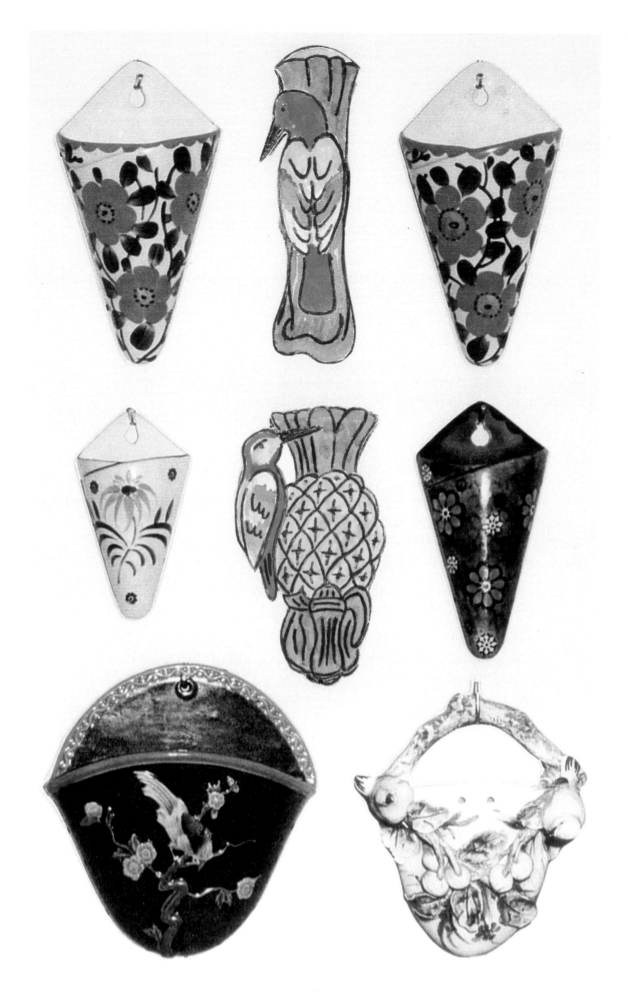

ENGLAND

England has a reputation for making beautiful pottery and porcelain since the 1700's. Many hundreds of factories have made thousands of different types of pottery and porcelain pieces over the years, and some are still producing today.

ROW 1:

1. Cupid, pink rose design, gold trim, marked with brown ink stamp "Maryleigh © HANDCRAFTED IN ENGLAND", 7 1/2" tall.   **$30 - 40**

2. Vase type wall pocket, 8 1/4" tall, black crocus pattern (chintz), marked "Royal Winton", made in Stoke, Staffordshire, England, 1900 to present (1986 Kovel's). No other information found.   **$995 - 1500**

3. Yellow and green leaves, marked with black ink stamp "KENSINGTON KPH ENGLAND". Made by Kensington Pottery LTD. of Hanley, England, 1922 to present, 8 1/2" tall.   **$85 - 100**

ROW 2:

1. Multicolored flowers, 7 1/2" tall, marked with green ink stamp "Radford England Handpainted". Possibly made by Samuel Radford LTD., of Fenton, Staffordshire, England, 1879-1957.   **$100 - 110**

2. Angel with a crown, gold trim, 9 3/4" tall. Marked with a blue ink stamp "7942", possibly England.   **$75 - 100**

3. Green shell, 6 1/2" tall, marked with blue ink stamp "Burlington WARE MADE IN ENGLAND".   **$75 - 85**

ROW 3:

1. Same pocket as row 1, no. 1, with different flower decals, same mark.   **$30 - 40**

2. Green with wicker, majolica, 10 1/2" tall. The owner identified this as made by Joseph Holdcroft, Longton, England, 1870-1920's. *An outstanding piece.*   **$1000 - 1500**

3. Brown painted country scene, marked with green ink stamp "Royal Staffordshire Ceramics MADE IN ENGLAND DESIGNED BY R.Y. COODDEN-16 A", 9" tall.   **$75 - 100**

FRANKOMA POTTERY

       Frankoma Pottery was started in Norman, Oklahoma in 1933 by John Frank and his wife Grace Lee. John taught art at the University of Oklahoma from 1927 until 1936. At that time he decided to devote full time to the pottery, producing utility art ware. In 1938 the pottery was moved to Sapulpa, Oklahoma, where it remains in operation today. Although the Franks no longer own the pottery, their daughter Joniece still does some designing for the new owners.

ROW 1:

    1. Phoebe Head, prairie green, no markings. Identified as   **$125 - 150**
       Frankoma. This piece has original price on the back,
       $1.75 each. Made of Ada clay.

    2. Phoebe Head, prairie green, mark impressed "FRANKOMA", and   **$125 - 150**
       also incised "730 C P.M.", made of Ada clay. This piece is
       heavier in weight than the one on the left.

ROW 2:

    Wagon Wheel, prairie green, impressed "94 Y FRANKOMA",   **$40 - 50**
    made of Ada clay.

ROW 3:

    1. Phoebe Head, black, no markings. Identified as Frankoma,   **$125 - 150**
       made of Ada clay.

    2. Acorn, white, mark in raised letters "FRANKOMA 190",   **$35 - 40**
       made of Sapulpa clay.

       Phoebe wall pockets were made in three different periods, 1948-1949 #730-I, reissued in 1951-1952 #194, then again in 1973-1975 #130. Frankoma made a few hand-painted Phoebe's but the only ones we have seen were at the Frankoma Pottery (not for sale). The hand painted Phoebe's face and neck are not glazed, but the hair is.

NOTE:

The colors of clay used in Frankoma pottery. Ada clay (light tan) 1933-1954. Sapulpa clay (brick red) 1955-1980's. Reddish pink 1980's - present, they started using an additive to make the clay stronger in the 1980's, which makes it a pinkish color.

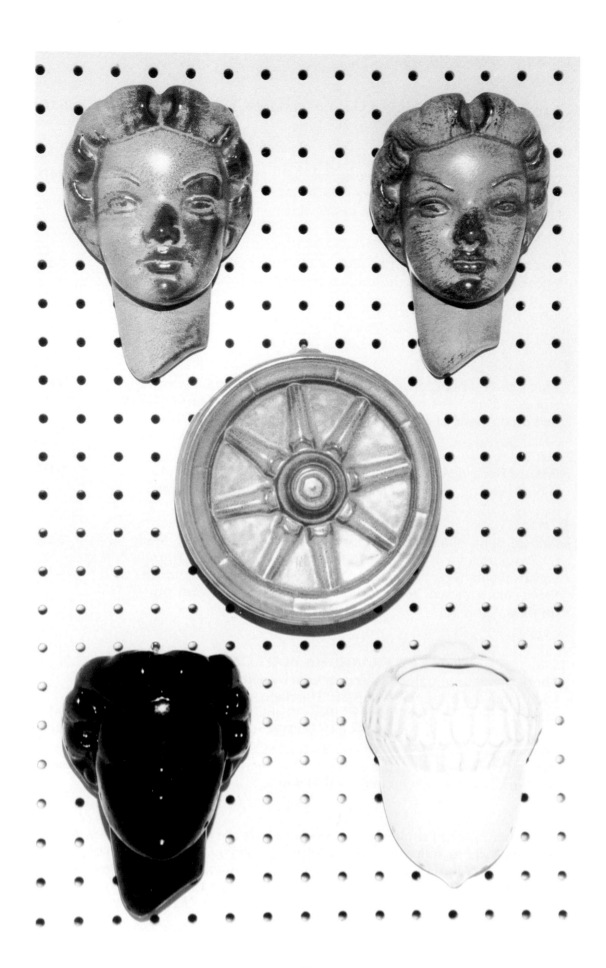

Frankoma Pottery

ROW 1:

1. Tiny Cowboy Boot, prairie green, no markings, made of Ada clay. Frankoma catalog #507. **$15 - 20**

2. Cowboy Boot, white, no marking, we call these "The picture boot". This one has a picture of "REBA McENTIRE" on it, (story below), (made from the newer clay). **$40 - 50**

3. Cowboy Boot, flame, mark impressed "FRANKOMA 133". These boots came in right and left pattern and various colors. **$35 - 40**

ROW 2:

1. Tiny Cowboy Boot, desert gold, no markings. It has a star design embossed near the top of the boot, and also has a leather thong tied on it. Made of Sapulpa clay. Frankoma catalog #507. **$10 - 15**

2. Picture Boot, desert gold, no markings. Made by Frankoma for H & H Glazing, Sapulpa, Oklahoma, (made from newer clay). **$15 - 20**

3. Picture Boot, black, no markings, (made from new clay). Made by Frankoma for H & H Glazing, Sapulpa, Oklahoma. These picture boots were a special order and were only made in the three colors shown. You can have any picture you want put on them. **$15 - 20**

HOW THE FRANKOMA BOOT CAME TO BE

There was a man named Harrison who owned a shoe store in Sapulpa, Oklahoma for 45 years. When Mr. Harrison's son (Bob) was small he took one of his cowboy boots to John Frank (they were friends) and asked him to make a mold of his son's boot. This was the start of the Frankoma boot as we know it today. Of course that was many years ago, and now the son is grown and is the owner of H & H Glazing along with his partner Mr. Sam Houghton, who told us this story.

The other known Frankoma wall pockets that are not in this book or our first book are as follows: Biliken figure 7", Cowboy boot 5", Dutch shoe #913 - 8 1/2", Indian head plain 3", Indian head with full head dress 4", leaves #196 - 12", Negro head 2 1/2", Ram's head #193 - 6", Wall pocket with birds as handles 5", and a wall pocket with waterer #A1 - 4 1/2" wide.

GERMANY

Wall pockets made in Germany are very hard to research because of the many different marks and factories. They made some of the most beautiful and unique wall pockets we have. They are hard to find, but certainly worth the hunt.

ROW 1:

Green Grapes and Leaves, multicolored in soft pastel greens, browns and pink, marked with blue ink stamp "Royal Bayreuth - T in a shield - 1794 BAVARIA", also impressed "Deponiert and circle".

$350 - 400

NOTE:

Royal Bayreuth is the name of a factory that was founded in Tettau, Bavaria, in 1794. It has continued until modern times. The marks have changed through the years. A stylized crest, the name Royal Bayreuth, and the word Bavaria appear in slightly different forms from 1870 to about 1919. Later pieces may include the words U.S. Zone, the year of issue, or the word Germany instead of Bavaria.

ROW 2:

1 and 2.

Flying Duck and Marsh Grass, marked with black ink stamp "Rosen (crown-seal) thal GERMANY KUNSTABTEILUNG SELS". and it also has a paper label "Rosen (crown seal) thale WELTMARKE DES PORZELLANS". Written with a lead pencil on the back of each piece is the original selling price of $69.50. There is no indication of when or where they were sold.

$150 - 175 ea.

NOTE:

Phillip Rosenthal started the manufacturing of fine Rosenthal porcelain at Selb, Bavaria in 1879 and it has continued until the present decade. Please note the ink stamp on the back of the above pieces is plainly marked "SELBS GERMANY". Some history books show it as "SELS BAVARIA". Which is right?? After 1871 the word GERMANY was commonly used along with BAVARIA.

Germany

ROW 1:

    1. Heart shape with spiral ornamental scroll design, multicolor   **$30 - 35**
        brown, with raised marks "61" and "Germany".

    2. Green pitcher trimmed with gold, raised marks "TWO HOUSES",   **$30 - 35**
        "¢", and "458", and it also has a paper label on the front that reads
        "GARSTENS TONNIESHOF QUALITAT, WEST GERMANY". This
        piece has no hole in the back for hanging, and has flat mold marks
        on the back so it will lay flat against the wall. It probably had a gold
        colored cord fastened to the handle to hang it by.

ROW 2:

    1. Bird and berries, mark impressed "8309". The style, markings   **$30 - 35**
        and mold marks on this piece has the distinctive characteristics
        of our other Germany marked wall pockets.

    2. Swallow and bird house, marked with black ink stamp   **$30 - 35**
        "GERMANY", and also an incised "10156".

    3. Bird and nest, mark impressed "902". The numbers have the   **$30 - 35**
        distinctive German style, they also have a red ink stamp
        that is impossible to read because it was applied into the
        side of the mold mark. (It looks like "GERMANY EAST").

ROW 3:

    1. Dark multicolor, marked with silver colored foil label "Keramik",   **$30 - 35**
        and also impressed "737". Hung by a gold colored cord.

    2. Large brown wise old owl, mark impressed "GERMANY",   **$80 - 90**
        and "1913".

    3. Black and tan with white stripes, marked with the same kind   **$30 - 35**
        of markings as #1 and hung by a gold colored cord.

Germany

ROW 1:

1. Double, gold trimmed, marked with a paper label "BAY (crown) KRISTALL KERAMIK", and incised "GERMANY 321", made by Edward Bay of Ransback, Rhineland, Germany, 1933 – present.   **$40 - 50**

2. Nude Lady, mark incised "9048-47 Germany".   **$125 - 150**

3. Old Boat, mark impressed "3930 Germany".   **$40 - 50**

ROW 2:

1. Brown/Ivory, mark impressed "2107". This is a Schafer and Vater, the company started in 1890 by Gustav Schafer and Gunther Vater at Volkstedt-Rudolstadt, Germany, closed in 1962.   **$125 - 150**

2. Lady/shell, mark incised "8922 Germany".   **$75 - 100**

3. Blue/white, mark impressed "2109". Identified as Schafer and Vater.   **$125 - 150**

ROW 3:

1. Multicolored with gold trim, mark impressed "726 Germany".   **$30 - 40**

2. Green with pink flowers/butterfly, mark impressed "6203-2". This came from a family from Germany.   **$60 - 80**

3. Double, gold trim, has a picture of a castle and the words "Suedberg in Hessen" on front and also impressed on the back "617 GERMANY".   **$60 - 75**

ROW 4: Doves on a basket, mark impressed "27918 (crown) S", with four hash marks on it. Made by Sitzendorf Porcelain Company, of Sitzendorf, Thuringia, Germany, 1845 to present.   **$175 - 225**

NOTE:

Most of the German wall pockets that are hung by gold colored cords, have a small solid brass clip applied at each end of the cord.

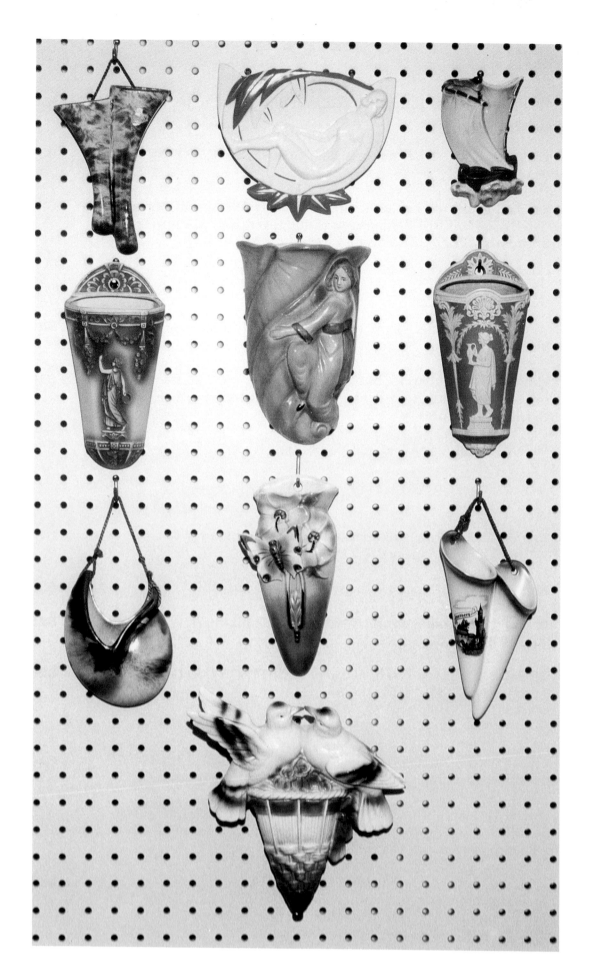

Germany

ROW 1:

1. Heart with birds, 4" tall, marked with blue ink stamp "Vv",   **$25 - 30**
    it also has an incised "SU 23/0".

2. Bag with heart, 4 1/2" tall, marked "Goebel", and "VP-80"   **$50 - 75**
    (Full Bee).

3. Double, gold trim, has a picture of last Royal House of Germany   **$25 - 35**
    "HOHEIZOLLIERN" Koblenz, on Rhine River, S.E. of Bonn, mark
    impressed "7217 GERMANY", 7 1/2".

ROW 2:

1. Woman with hunter, 4 1/2" tall, mark incised "W301", and also   **$30 - 40**
    black ink stamped "HANDWORK MADE IN AUSTRIA".

2. Fan shape with flowers, butterfly and crane, 12" tall, no markings,   **$1800 - 2200**
    priced and identified by dealer as Dresden China from Dresden,
    Germany, mid-1800's.

3. Man/mandolin, size and mark same as #1.   **$30 - 40**

ROW 3:

1. Parrot/basket, 81/4" tall, marked with red ink stamp   **$75 - 95**
    "GERMANY", also incised "5218-1".

2. Blue Peacock, 5", mark is incised "4021 GERMANY".   **$30 - 40**

3. Round with handles, country scene, 4 1/2" tall, mark is incised   **$25 - 30**
    "DYBBOL-MOLLE GERMANY".

4. Girl, Boy and Bird, 4" tall, marked "HANITZSCH 300 GERMANY".   **$25 - 30**

ROW 4:

1&2. Cherub sitting on a cornucopia, 7 3/4". The side view shows   **$100 - 175**
      the blue ink stamp mark "NR GERMANY", maker unknown.

3. Parrot with gold beak, 7 3/4" tall, marked with green ink stamp   **$75 - 95**
    "☆ RS (wreath) GERMANY". Made by Reinhold Schlegelmilch of
    Tillowitz, Silesia, Germany, 1869-1938.

4 & 5. Back and front view of Red-Cap / Bellboy, 61/4" tall, has two   **$75 - 125**
        openings, one in flowers and one in his head, mark incised "WG
        (crown bee) T608", and also a blue ink stamp "WG (crown bee)
        GERMANY R", made by Goebel about 1935.

55

GLASS

Glass wall pockets were first produced in the late 1800's and as shown in this chapter are still being made in the late 1900's. The U.S. Glass, Fostoria, Westmoreland and Imperial are a few of the older companies that made some beautiful wall pockets, car vases and match holders. Also note the new glass wall pockets made for Tiara Exclusives, by Fenton Art Glass in 1995 from the old Imperial molds.

ROW 1:

    1. Clear Glass Woodpecker, no markings, made by Diamond   **$50 - 60**
Glass-Ware Company, Indiana, Pennsylvania.

    2. Pink Depression Glass Woodpecker, no markings, made by   **$50 - 60**
Diamond Glass-Ware Company, Indiana, Pennsylvania.

ROW 2:

    Marigold Carnival Glass Woodpecker, no markings, was made by   **$100 - 125**
Northwood Glass Company. When Northwood went out of business, pieces of the woodpecker were only found in the marigold color in the diggings behind the old Northwood Glass factory.

ROW 3:

    1. Black Amethyst Glass Woodpecker, no markings, appears black   **$50 - 60**
until held in a bright light, then a deep purple can be seen. Made by Diamond Glass-Ware Company at Indiana, Pennsylvania.

    2. Green Depression Glass Woodpecker, no markings, glows bright   **$50 - 60**
under a black light. Made by Diamond Glass Company at Indiana, Pennsylvania.

NOTE:

In 1891 the Indiana Glass Company began production at a plant in Indiana, Pennsylvania. The plant changed owners three more times before finally burning to the ground in 1931. In 1897 the Northwood Glass Works moved into the factory (Northwood is known for it's carnival glass). When Northwood moved on, it became Dugan Glass, then later it changed to the Diamond Glass Company. This could explain the many different opinions of who made the woodpecker wall pocket.

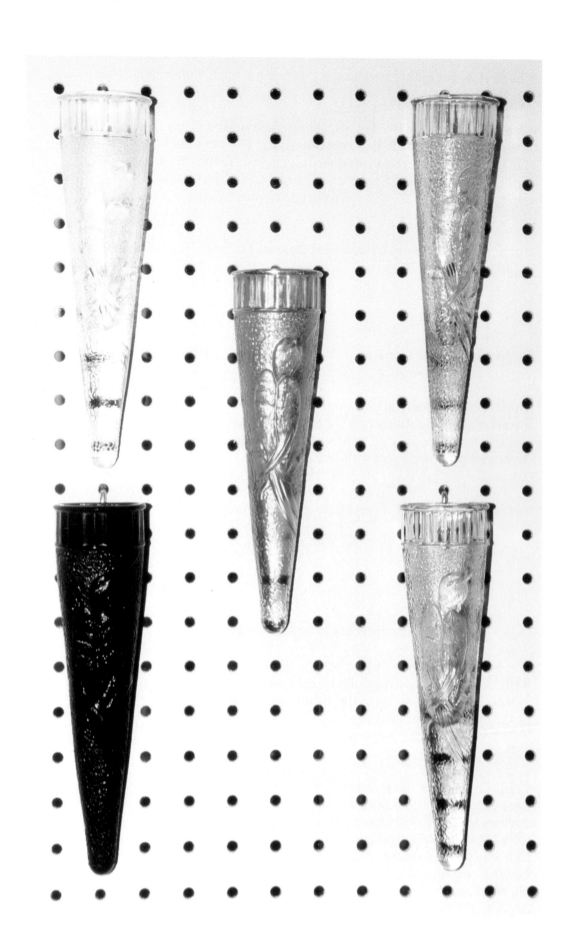

Glass

ROW 1:

1. Peach colored glass, basket and flower pattern. Tiara Exclusives. **$30 - 40**

2. Green Boot Match Holder, rough surface on front to strike match **$4 - 8**
   on, no markings, this is a reproduction. The originals
   (DEGENHART) were marked with a raised "D in a ♥" and made
   by Crystal Art Glass Company, Cambridge, Ohio, 1947-1978.
   An original piece marked "DEGENHART". – **$25 - 65**

3. Spruce Green Glass, basket and flowers pattern, Tiara Exclusives. **$30 - 40**

ROW 2:

1. Black (amethyst) glass with crackle design, no markings. **$35 - 45**

2. Multicolored glass ash receiver with metal bracket, (used in **$50 - 60**
   automobiles), no markings. This piece glows fluorescent under
   a black light because of uranium used in the glass.
   (Information page in back of book).

3. Yellow (vaseline) glass, scroll design, no markings, made by **$50 - 75**
   U.S. Glass.

ROW 3:

1. Clear glass horn, no markings, maker unknown. **$30 - 40**

2. White milk glass with applied orange color, trimmed with hand **$35 - 50**
   painted black lines, unusual mold design, no markings,
   possibly Czechoslovakian.

NOTE:

Tiara Exclusives were formed in 1970, the product is a selection of decorative and tableware items produced for the exclusive sale to customers through independent associates. The two wall pockets in row 1, were made by Fenton Art Glass from Imperial Glass molds that were acquired when Lancaster Colony Corp. bought Imperial Glass Company in 1984. Tiara is a subsidiary of Lancaster Colony. Mr. Bill Fenton has verified that Fenton Art Glass made the wall pockets for Tiara Exclusives. (Tiara discontinued the wall pockets shown on this page June 30, 1996).

Glass

ROW 1:

    1. Canoe, yellow (vaseline) glass, daisy and button pattern,   **$60 - 80**
no markings, maker unknown.

ROW 2:

    1. Clear satin finish Tiffin, with hand-painted (lily of the   **$100 - 125**
valley) flowers, style #320, 9 1/8" long x 3 3/8" wide.

    2. Clear plain Tiffin, style #320, 9 1/8" long x 3 3/8" wide.   **$60 - 80**

    3. Green satin finish Tiffin, with a black line painted around   **$60 - 80**
the rim, style #320, 9 1/8" long x 3 3/8" wide.

ROW 3:

    1. Clear Fostoria trimmed with etched floral design, style #1881,   **$60 - 75**
8 1/4" long x 3" wide.

    2. White Milk Glass Whisk Broom, marked with raised letters "IG".   **$75 - 100**
It also has a blue foil label "Imperial U.S.A. GENUINE MILK
GLASS".

    3. Clear plain Fostoria, style #1881, 8 1/4" long x 3" wide.   **$50 - 60**

NOTE:

Imperial Glass Company began producing in 1904 in Bellaire, Ohio, making pressed tableware. In 1958 Imperial bought most of the mold equipment from the Heisey Glass Factory in Newark, Ohio. They also bought molds from the Cambridge Glass Company in 1960. Lenox, Incorporated, bought the Imperial plant in 1972 and operated it under the name "New Imperial Corporation" until 1984, when it was sold again to the Lancaster Colony Corporation. "Tiara Exclusives" is a division of Lancaster Colony Corporation, and has access to the Imperial molds.

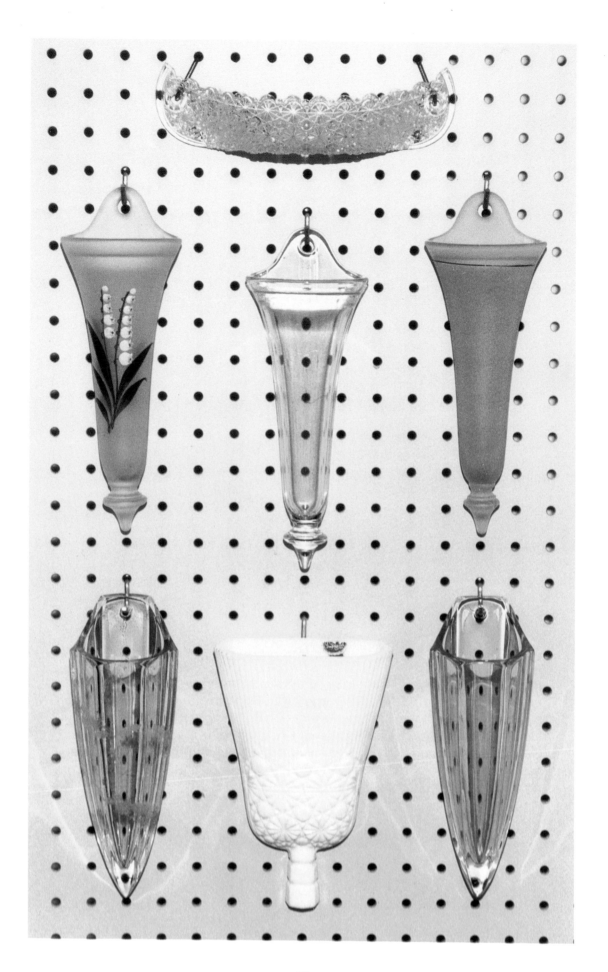

61

Glass

ROW 1:

    1. Green Satin Tiffin, style #16258, 9 1/4" long x 3 7/8" wide.   **$65 - 100**

    2. Black Satin Tiffin, style #16258, 9 1/4" long x 3 7/8" wide.   **$65 - 100**

    3. Light Blue Satin Tiffin, style #16258, 9 1/4" long x 3 7/8" wide.   **$65 - 100**

ROW 2:

    1. Amethyst Satin Tiffin, style #16258, 9 1/4" long x 3 7/8" wide.   **$65 - 100**

    2. Amber Satin Tiffin, style #16258, 9 1/4" long x 3 7/8" wide.   **$65 - 100**

    3. Royal Blue Satin Tiffin, style #16258, 9 1/4" long x 3 7/8" wide.   **$65 - 100**

NOTE:

Tiffin was one among many glass companies comprising the U.S. Glass Company. Located in Tiffin, Ohio, the Tiffin Company made quality blown stemware and delicately pressed dinnerware, along with some very unique wall pockets. Tiffin wall pockets are probably the most readily available of the glass wall pockets we find, but as shown in this chapter, they are also some of the most beautiful and high quality and well worth collecting, if you can find them.

Glass

ROW 1:

    1. Black Tiffin, glossy and satin finish, trimmed with gold, style #320, 9 1/8" long x 3 3/8" wide. Tiffin called this pattern "Echel Finish".   **$75 - 100**

    2. Black Satin Tiffin, style #320, 9 1/8" long x 3 3/8" wide.   **$60 - 80**

    3. Black Tiffin, glossy and satin finish with vertical stripes, style #320, 9 1/8" long x 3 3/8" wide. Tiffin called this pattern "Satin Ribbon".   **$125 - 175**

ROW 2:

    1. Royal blue satin Tiffin, style #320, 9 1/8" long x 3 3/8" wide.   **$60 - 80**

    2. Canary Yellow Satin Tiffin, style #320, 9 1/8" long x 3 3/8" wide.   **$60 - 80**

    3. Light Blue Satin Tiffin, style #320, 9 1/8" long x 3 3/8" wide.   **$60 - 80**

ROW 3:

    1. Tiffin, red with a brilliant finish, style #320, 9 1/8" long x 3 3/8" wide.   **$75 - 100**

    2. Pink Satin Tiffin with hand-painted flowers, style #320, 9 1/8" long x 3 3/8" wide.   **$100 - 125**

    3. Green Satin Tiffin, style #320, 9 1/8" long x 3 3/8" wide.   **$60 - 80**

NOTE;

There are Tiffin Glass wall pockets that are trimmed with applied metals, pearls and other semi-precious stones. It is not clear whether these were decorated at the glass factory, sent out to a jobber or done after they had been sold to an individual.

Glass

ROW 1:

    1. Blue Fostoria, style #1881, 8 1/4" long x 3" wide.   **$50 - 75**

    2. Green Fostoria, style #1881, 8 1/4" long x 3" wide.   **$125 - 150**
        This piece has a double collectable value because it
        has the "MASONIC EMBLEM" applied in gold leaf.

    3. Black Fostoria, style #1881, 81/4" long x 3" wide.   **$50 - 75**

ROW 2:

    1. Amber Fostoria, trimmed with silver inlay floral decoration,   **$100 - 125**
        style #1881, 8 1/4" long x 3" wide.

    2. Clear Fostoria, with etched floral design, style #1881,   **$75 - 100**
        8 1/4" long x 3" wide.

    3. Green Fostoria, trimmed with silver inlay floral decoration,   **$100 - 125**
        style #1881, 8 1/4" long x 3" wide.

NOTES:

Fostoria Glass Company began in Fostoria, Ohio in 1887 but moved to Moundsville, West Virginia in 1891 when fuel supplies ran short. Best known for the oil lamps they made in the early years, Fostoria is also well known for their glassware. In 1983 The Fostoria Company was sold to the Lancaster Colony Corporation and is still in operation today. The glassware being made today can be easily identified from the older pieces. According to the employees at a retail outlet in our area, Fostoria no longer makes wall pockets.

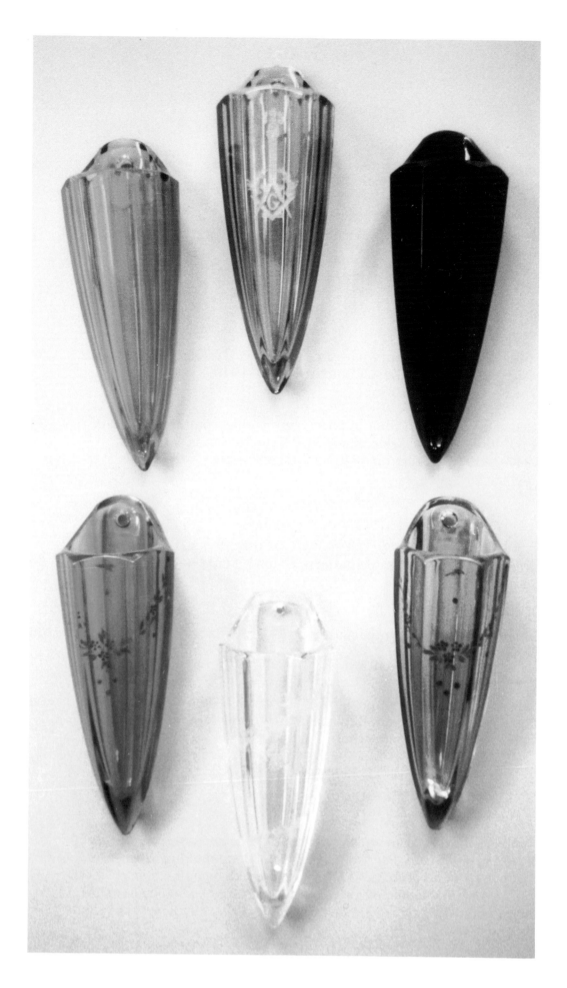

Glass

ROW 1:

1. Blue glass hand-blown morning glory, 7 3/4" long, no markings, maker unknown. **$20 - 40**

2. Green glass hand-blown morning glory, 7 3/4" long, no markings, maker unknown. **$20 - 40**

ROW 2:

1. Pink Glass, "anniversary pattern", #2930, 6 1/2" long x 3 1/2" wide. Made by Jeannette Glass Company, 1947-1949. **$40 - 50**

2. Clear glass with red color applied, "anniversary pattern", #2930, 6 1/2" long x 3 1/2" wide. Made by Jeannette Glass Company, 1947-1949. See story on Jeannette Glass below. **$40 - 50**

ROW 3:

1. Green glass, beaded grape pattern, 6" long. Made by U.S. Glass Company. **$40 - 50**

2. Green glass, beaded grape pattern, 10" long. Made by U.S. Glass Company. **$50 - 75**

3. Green glass, beaded grape pattern, 6" long. Made by U.S. Glass Company. These three wall pockets are completely round, not flat on the back side where the hole is. **$40 - 50**

Price per set of three **$130 - 175**

NOTE:

Jeannette Glass Company started out as a bottle factory in the early 1900's in Jeannette, Pennsylvania. They began making tableware in the early 1920's and over the many years of production have made a wide range of kitchen items, including water sets, mixing bowls, reamers, punch bowl sets, etc., along with the wall pockets shown on this page and car vases.

Glass

ROW 1:

    1. Black Amethyst Glass Owl on tree branch with green leaves, all molded into glass, 6 1/2" long x 4" wide. This was originally cold painted, but most of the paint is gone. No markings and maker unknown.   **$75 - 100**

    2. White Milk Glass, made by the Westmoreland Glass Company, pattern is "Panelled Grape", 5" long x 8" wide, and also made in 6" wide size. See comments at bottom of page on Westmoreland Glass Company.   **$175 - 200**

ROW 2:

    Amber Glass, ribbed pattern, 5 1/2" long x 10 1/2" wide. This piece has the "ART-DECO" style, probably hung in a theater or funeral parlor. It has a permanent water mark inside indicating it was used. No markings and maker unknown.   **$60 - 80**

ROW 3:

    1. Peacock blue colored glass, trimmed with gold decoration which includes little clear glass beads applied over the gold, giving this piece a finish that is uneven, 6 1/2" long x 4" wide. No markings and maker unknown, possibly Czechoslovakia.   **$125 - 150**

    2. Royal blue colored glass, applied over clear glass, hand-painted decoration of cornucopia with multicolored flowers, 8 1/2" long x 5 3/4" wide. No markings and maker unknown, possibly Czechoslovakia.   **$100 - 125**

NOTE:

The Westmoreland Specialty Company began producing glass at Grapeville, Pennsylvania in 1890, and later changed the name to The Westmoreland Glass Company. During WWI they made the glass candy containers that are so collectable today. They made some very nice wall pockets and closed in 1984.

Glass

ROW 1:

    1. White Milk Glass with scroll design, 6" long x 5" wide,   **$50 - 80**
       no markings, made by U.S.Glass Company.

    2. Blue Glass with scroll design, 6" long x 5" wide, no   **$50 - 80**
       markings, made by U.S. Glass Company. These were also
       made in green and canary yellow as well as with a satin
       finish.

ROW 2:

    1. White Milk Glass with unusual mold design, hand-painted   **$40 - 60**
       blue with other decorations, 6 1/8" long x 4 3/4" wide.
       No markings, possibly Czechoslovakian.

    2. Orange Glass with black trim, 7 1/8" long x 4" wide. No   **$40 - 60**
       markings, identified as Czechoslovakia.

    3. Marigold Carnival Color, crackle finish, 5 7/8" long x   **$35 - 50**
       5 3/8" wide. No markings and maker unknown.

ROW 3:

    1. Clear Glass with satin finish, vertical ribbed design, 5 7/8" long   **$35 - 50**
       x 5 3/8" wide. No markings and maker unknown.

    2. Green Glass, vertical ribbed design, 5 7/8" long x 5 3/8" wide.   **$35 - 50**
       No markings and maker unknown.

NOTE:

The United States Glass Company was formed by 18 different glass companies in 1891. They were scattered all over Pennsylvania, Ohio and West Virginia. Most of the glass companies shut down or moved on to other areas over the years and in 1938 the main offices were moved to Tiffin, Ohio. Only the Pittsburgh plant and the Tiffin plant were still operating by that time. By 1962, U.S. Glass Company was gone and only Tiffin Glass Company remained. It finally closed in 1980. The wall pockets in row 1 on this page were made by U.S. Glass Company, the other three that are similar were not, on close examination the size, shape and design are different.

Glass

ROW 1:

1. Green Glass, hand-blown, decorated with hand-painted flowers,   **$110 - 135**
   7 3/4" long x 4 3/8" wide, no markings. In a 1930 catalog from the
   Butler Brothers National Distributor of General Merchandise,
   St. Louis, Mo., it shows this wall pocket as imported from
   Czechoslovakia, #IC-6068. The thin blown glass, cut and polished
   top, sold for $7.20 per dozen, and also came in amber glass.

2. Clear Glass Horn, 11 3/4" long, no markings and maker unknown.   **$40 - 50**

ROW 2:

1. Amber Glass with unusual mold design, 6 1/2" long x 5 1/4" wide.   **$100 - 125**
   No markings, possibly Czechoslovakian.

2. Green Glass with unusual mold design, 6 1/2" long x 5 1/4" wide.   **$100 - 125**
   No markings, possibly Czechoslovakian.

ROW 3:

1. Green Satin Glass Tiffin with hand-painted red and black "parrot"   **$135 - 160**
   design, style #320, 9 1/2" long x 3 3/8" wide. This was listed on a
   1926 U.S. Glass Catalog page.

2. White Milk Glass, basket with flower pattern, 6" long x 4" wide,   **$75 - 100**
   marked with black and silver label "ORIGINAL DOE SKIN FINISH",
   also marked with a blue foil label "Imperial U.S.A. GENUINE
   MILK GLASS", 1901 - 1972.

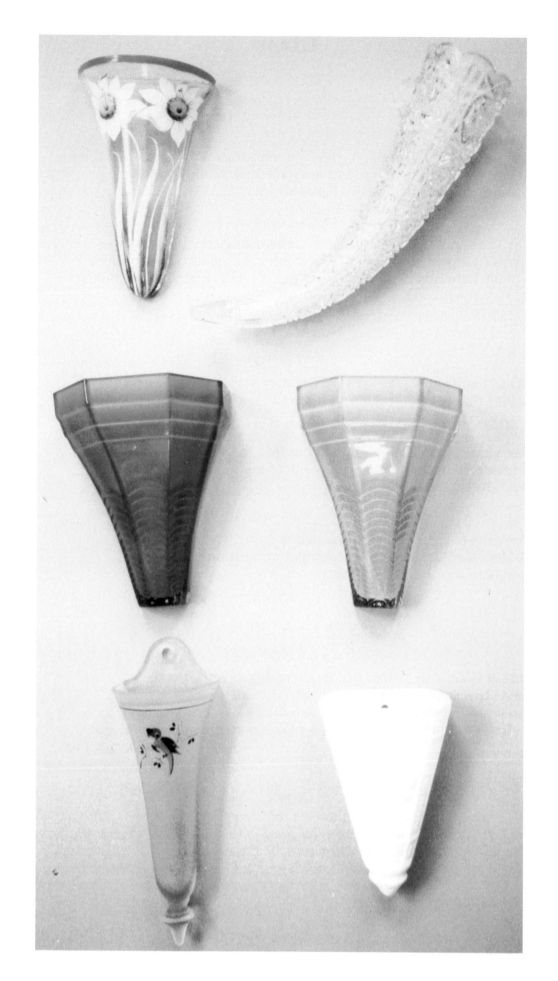

Glass

ROW 1:

    1. Car Vase, yellow (vaseline) glass, no markings. This piece has the   **$50 - 75**
bottom tip broken off, ground and polished. Made by McKee
Glass Company, Jeannette, Pennsylvania.

    2. Car Vase, yellow (vaseline) glass, no markings, made by McKee   **$85 - 100**
Glass Company. Both of the above car vases glow bright under
a black light and originally came with a nickle plated metal holder.

ROW 2:

    1. Rooter, large grey glass vase, in a fancy scroll wrought iron   **$35 - 50**
holder painted gold color, not marked.

    2. Car Vase, clear glass with hand cut design, no markings on glass.   **$75 - 85**
A nickle plated metal holder attached, mark stamped into metal
"PAT. APLD. FOR".

    3. Rooter, two clear crackle glass vases, hung from two metal   **$25 - 30**
holders that are attached to a small wood simulated door,
complete with hinges and latch.

ROW 3:

Pair of Glass Car Vases, marigold crackle glass pattern,
made by Jeannette Glass Company, Jeannette, Pennsylvania.
In the 1925 catalog these were listed as #5265 in the amber
iridescent color and came with a nickle plated metal holder.

Price per each – **$75 - 85**

NOTE:

*Often glass wall pockets, car vases and cemetery vases are confused. Wall
pockets almost always have a flat back with a hole for hanging. Car vases
usually had a metal holder that attached to the inside of the car, many of
the metal holders are missing when you find a car vase. (With holder add
$15.00 to $25.00). Cemetery vases have a sharp pointed end for pushing
into the ground.*

Glass

ROW 1:

1. Rooter, clear crackle glass vase with metal holder with blue flower. No markings and maker unknown. **$12 - 15**

2. Rooter, clear glass vase, ivory colored metal mesh holder, no markings and maker unknown. **$12 - 15**

3. Rooter, clear frosted glass vase with hand-painted flowers and a metal holder, no markings and maker unknown. **$12 - 15**

4. Rooter, clear crackle glass vase, metal holder with green ship. No markings and maker unknown. **$12 - 15**

ROW 2:

Rooter, two green glass vases, marked with silver foil labels on vases that read "ANOTHER PLANTERS Creation PATENT APPLIED FOR, PLANTERS & NOVELTIES, N.Y.C., 57, N.Y.", in metal holder. **$15 - 20**

ROW 3:

1. Rooter, large marigold colored glass vase, in a fancy scroll, wrought iron holder painted gold color, no markings and maker unknown. **$35 - 50**

2. Rooter, green glass vase, metal holder, no markings and maker unknown **$12 - 15**

3. Rooter, large marigold colored glass vase, information same as #1.
Price per pair – **$75 - 100**

NOTE:

Glass rooters were used to root ivy or other plants in water or for fresh flowers.

Glass

ROW 1:

1. Carnival Glass, marigold color, crackle finish, 5 3/4" tall, no markings and maker unknown.   **$40 - 50**

2. Clear Glass with yellow applied paint, 6 1/2", anniversary pattern #2930, made by Jeanette Glass Company, 1947-1949.   **$40 - 50**

3. Ivory colored glass (alacite), made by Aladdin Lamp Company, 8 1/2" tall.   **$75 - 100**

ROW 2:

1. Amber Glass, appears to be handmade, 10" tall, no markings and maker unknown. Owner says it is possibly Czechoslovakian.   **$65 - 75**

2. Blue Glass Fiddle with a metal hanger, no markings, unidentified, 8".   **$30 - 35**

ROW 3:

1. White Milk Glass with applied green, trimmed with black lines, 6" tall, no markings, possibly Czechoslovakian.   **$35 - 50**

2. Cobalt blue and clear glass, handmade, 9" tall, no markings. This piece was bought in Germany at a small glass factory by our friend Viola. She saw it hanging on a post the first time she was there, forgot to buy it, two years later she went back, the wall pocket was still hanging there (of course she bought it).   **$65 - 85**

3. Clear glass with a frosted finish, vertical panels design, 6 1/2" tall, no markings and maker unknown.   **$30 - 35**

ROW 4:

1. Clear Crystal Glass with vertical lines design, marked with silver foil label "ASTRAL FULL LEAD HANDMADE CRYSTAL KOREA", 9 1/4" tall.   **$75 - 125**

2. Black (amethyst) glass, 7 1/4" tall, no markings and maker unknown.   **$85 - 100**

Glass

ROW 1:

1. Rooter, ruby red glass vase, metal wire holder with flower and leaf design. No markings and maker unknown. **$20 - 30**

2. Rooter, ruby red glass vase, flat metal and wire holder with scroll and leaf design. No markings and maker unknown. **$15 - 25**

3. Rooter, same as #1. Price per pair – **$40 - 60**

ROW 2:

1. Rooter, three cobalt blue glass vases with metal wire holder and a musical design. No markings and maker unknown. **$30 - 45**

2. Rooter, two cobalt blue glass vases, metal wire holder with scroll design. No markings and maker unknown. **$30 - 40**

ROW 3:

1. Rooter, long cobalt blue glass vase, flat metal holder with scroll and leaf design. No markings and maker unknown. **$30 - 45**

2. Rooter, long cobalt blue glass vase, metal wire holder with scroll design. No marking and maker unknown. **$30 - 45**

NOTE;

We have tried very hard to give you as much information as possible about glass wall pockets. We were very fortunate to have a lot of help from other collectors who were very happy to share their knowledge with us.

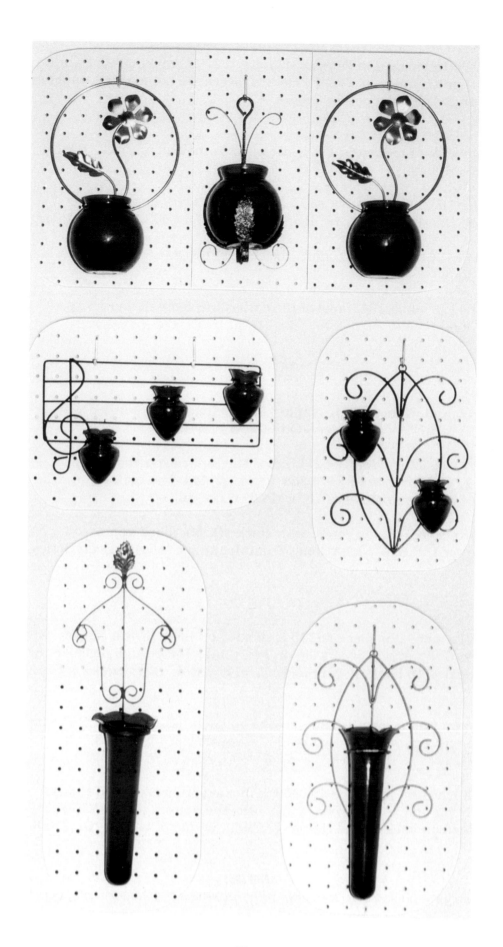

HAEGER POTTERY

Haeger Pottery began in Dundee, Illinois in 1871, making bricks and tiles. In 1904 they started making art pottery. So many of the Haeger pieces are not marked, which makes it very hard to identify from other American pottery pieces.

ROW 1:

1. Aqua leaf, #3112, circa 1941, the mark is molded on back "Haeger USA", 6" long. $25 - 30

2. Green "Bacchus" lavabo, #835, circa 1962, marked with paper label "Haeger Pottery", 13" long. This was in a 1962 Haeger catalog. $150 - 200

3. Blue #126, circa 1914, one of the earliest designs, no markings, 10" long. $90 - 100

4. Red #126, circa 1914, one of the earliest designs, no markings, 10" long. $90 - 100

ROW 2:

1. Green and white rocking cradle #917A, circa 1939, marked with paper label "Haeger Pottery, Dundee, IL.", 5" long. $15 - 20

2. Turquoise blue "Lion Head" lavabo. The top piece is molded on back "#R1504", size 9 1/4" wide x 14 1/2" tall. The bottom piece is not marked, size 16" wide x 6 1/4" tall. $200 - 250

3. Mauve color rocking cradle with stork #B649, mark impressed "Haeger © U.S.A.", 5 3/4" long. From the junior "All American Series". $10 - 15

ROW 3:

1. Tan Lavabo – top piece #8186 is molded on back "Royal Haeger © 8186 USA", and is 6 1/2" wide x 14 1/4" tall. The bottom piece #8187 is molded on back "Royal Haeger © 8187 USA", 12 1/4" wide x 5 1/4" tall. $25 - 30

2. A green wall pocket #R725, molded on back "Haeger 725 USA", and also has a paper label that reads "Royal Haeger", 5 1/8" tall. $25 - 30

3. Pink Lavabo – top piece #R1506 is molded on back "Royal Haeger R 1506", and is 6 3/4" wide x 13" tall. The bottom piece #R1507 is molded on back "Royal Haeger R 1507", and is 8" wide x 6 1/2" tall. $30 - 40

NOTE:
In our first book there are nine different styles of Haeger wall pockets shown.

A. 835   13" Bacchus Lavabo Urn $15.00
Leaf Green, Gold Tweed
Faience - $18.00

HULL POTTERY

Hull Pottery was started in Crooksville, Ohio in 1904 and continued until the mid-1980's making some of the most beautiful art pottery in history. Although they did not make a large number of wall pockets, what they did make is of the highest quality.

ROW 1:

    1. Bow-Knot pitcher, #B-26, turquoise and blue, late 1940's, mark raised letters "U.S.A. Hull Art B-26-6".   **$200 - 250**

    2. Bow-Knot pitcher #B-26, pink and blue, late 1940's, mark raised letters "U.S.A. Hull Art B-26-6", and also round silver foil label "HULL POTTERY CROOKSVILLE, OHIO".   **$200 - 250**

ROW 2:

    1. Woodland shell #W13, dark pink, late 1940's and early 1950's, mark with raised letters "W13-7$\frac{1}{2}$ Hull U.S.A.".   **$100 - 150**

    2. Butterfly lavabo, white, 1950's. The top is #B24 and the mark is incised "Hull B24". The bottom is #B25 and the mark is incised "Hull B25 USA © '56". This does not have the metal rack that both pieces hang on.   **$200 - 250**

    3. Woodland shell #W13, light pink, late 1940's and early 1950's, the mark is in raised letters "W13-7$\frac{1}{2}$ Hull U.S.A.".   **$100 - 150**

ROW 3:

    1. Ribbon bow #71, yellow and pink, 1950's. The mark is in raised letters "71 USA".   **$40 - 60**

    2. Sun Glow pitcher #81, glossy pink, early 1950's. The mark is incised "USA 81", and also has paper label "W. Woolworth Co.".   **$60 - 90**

NOTE:

In our first book the following wall pockets are shown, (they are not pictured in this second book), but we would like to list them for quick reference.

    Bow Knot cup and saucer #B-24, blue and pink.
    Bow Knot whisk broom #B-27, pink, blue and turquoise blue.
    Flying goose #67, blue and pink.
    Little Red Riding Hood, 9" tall.
    Sun Glow pitcher #81, glossy yellow.
    Sun Glow whisk broom #82, glossy yellow and glossy pink.
    Sun Glow cup and saucer #B24, glossy pink.
    Sun Glow iron #83, glossy pink.

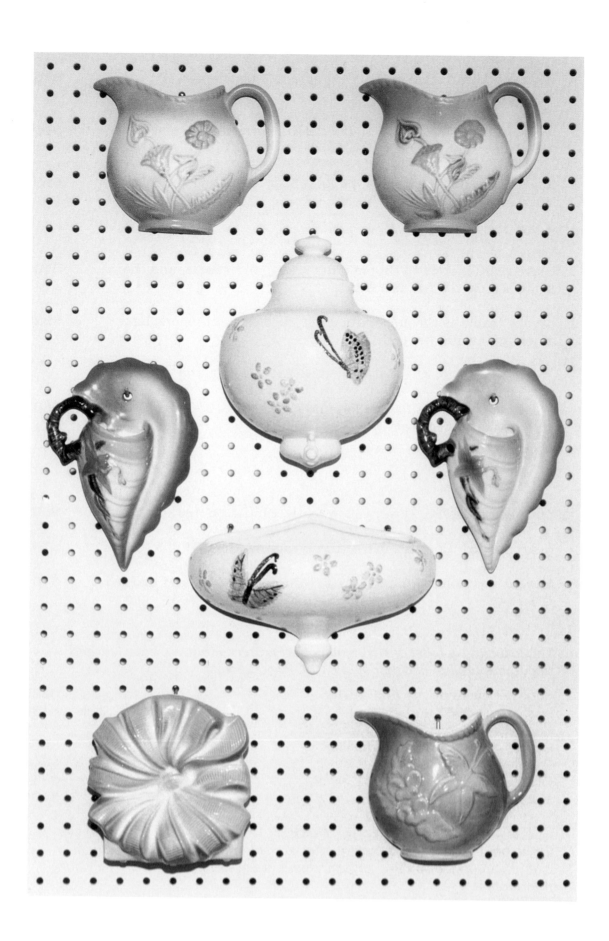

Hull Pottery

ROW 1:

    1. Royal Woodland shell #W13, turquoise, 1950's, is marked   **$75 - 100**
        "W13-7$1/2$ Hull U.S.A.".

    2. Woodland shell #W13, green, late 1940's early 1950's, marked   **$100 - 150**
        "W 13-7$1/2$ Hull U.S.A.".

    3. Royal Woodland shell #W13, pink, 1950's, is marked "W13-7$1/2$ **$75 - 100**
        Hull U.S.A.".

ROW 2:

    1. Leaves with berries #112, pink and green, mid 1950's, and the   **$50 - 75**
        mark is incised "Hull 112 USA".

    2. Lavabo (same as the one on the prior page except this one has   **$225 - 275**
        an original metal hanger).

ROW 3:

    Leaves and berries #112, yellow and green, mid 1950's,   **$50 - 75**
    and the mark is incised "Hull 112 USA".

ROW 4:

    1. Sun Glow iron #83, glossy yellow, early 1950's, no markings.   **$60 - 90**

    2. Heart shaped "Rosella", marked with raised letters "Hull R10 6$1/2$".   **$75 - 100**

    3. Mayfair mandolin #84, pink, 1960's through 1970's, and marked   **$40 - 60**
        "USA 84".

NOTE:

The following is a list of Hull wall pocket patterns that we have learned about, but are not in either of our Wall Pocket books.

Square Bow Knot cup and saucer	**$225 - 275**
Lusterware #507 and #508, 9".	Each – **$150 - 200**
Early art lusterware 8$1/2$", unmarked.	**$150 - 200**
Open Rose #125, 8$1/2$" (Camellia).	**$300 - 400**
Poppy #609, 9".	**$300 - 400**
Oval frame, "ATHENA", #611, 8$1/2$".	**$75 - 100**
Matte black with gold accents #120, 8".	**$100 - 150**

NOTE:

There are two other wall pockets that are said to be Hull. We have never seen them, so we can not confirm this, but we will include them for your information.

Violin #85, 7".	**$40 - 60**
Chinese man #120.	**$40 - 60**

89

HUMMEL

Berta Hummel was a budding artist even as a child in Massing, Bavaria. She attended art school at the Academy of Applied Arts in Munich, Bavaria in 1927 at the age of eighteen, graduating in 1931 at the age of 22. At that time she joined a Franciscan Convent, becoming a nun after the two years that it took to complete her Novitiate. The date was August 22, 1933. Her name then became Sister Maria Innocentia Hummel. She taught in a convent school. The first Hummel figurines came on the market in 1935 after Sister Hummel signed a contract with Goebel. All the money that was made from the Hummel figurines went to the convent. Sister Maria Innocentia Hummel died of tuberculosis in November 1946 at the age of 37, leaving over 500 original sketches. Hummel figurines are still being made today. The three wall pockets shown on the opposite page were introduced during the stylized bee era and are the only three patterns of wall pockets Hummel designed.

TOP:

       Boy in tree, #360-B, mark incised on front side under the boy   **$150 - 200**
       "M.I. Hummel", and also impressed on back "360/B" and "1958",
       with a blue ink stamp "© Goebel W. Germany".

MIDDLE:

       Boy and girl in tree, #360/A, mark incised on front side under   **$150 - 200**
       the girl "M.I. Hummel", and also impressed on back "360/A"
       and "1958", and a blue ink stamp "© Goebel W. Germany". This
       piece is signed in black by the artist "Mt 83".

BOTTOM:

       Girl in tree, #360/C, mark incised on front under girl "M.I. Hummel",   **$500 - 600**
       and also impressed on the back "360/C" and "© Goebel 1958", and a
       blue ink stamp "Stylized Bee W. Germany".

NOTE:

It is almost impossible to place a price on Hummel wall pockets, they are hard to find and usually priced according to what the dealer payed for them. As shown in our prices, the stylized bee mark commands a much higher price.

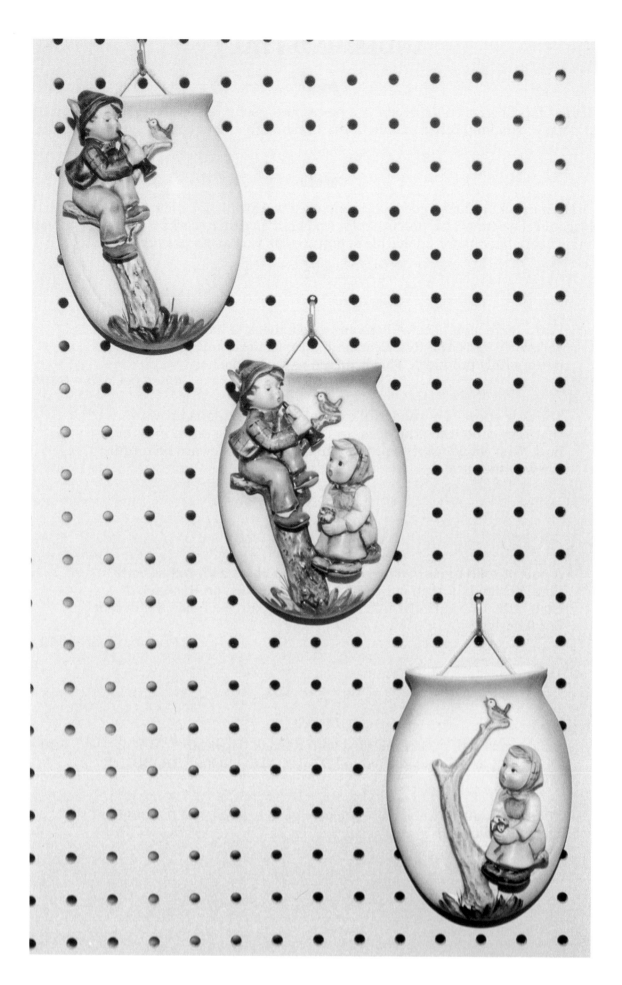

INDIA AND ITALY

India

Brass has been used for decorative pieces and useful tablewares since ancient times. It is an alloy of copper, zinc and other metals. India brass is the most collectable of the brass we find today.

Italy

Italian mass produced goods are renowned worldwide for their formal beauty, their brilliant coloring and their innovative talent. Color and light give their works a sense of exuberance and fantasy. Italy is very famous for its marble sculptures as well as its pottery.

ROW 1:

Extra large pink lilies with green leaves, mark is hand-painted in yellow "0193-ITALY-PV". Beautiful, a perfect example of the type of pottery Italy produces. This is a true pair of opposites.

Price per pair – **$150 - 200**

The pair above is a wonderful example of the fabulous art ware that Italy produced. The lilies have a deep opening down into the bud. Who would want to put anything in them, they are beautiful the way they are.

ROW 2:

A pair of solid brass wall pockets, painted black with red accents, floral design has been cut in. The mark is etched on the back of each "OX. 167. H.H. INDIA". This is a true pair, each has a different floral design.

Price per pair – **$40 - 50**

ROW 3:

Solid brass wall pocket, marked with a black paper label "MADE IN INDIA", and a gold colored foil label "GATCO SOLID BRASS".

$20 - 30

The three wall pockets above are very good examples of the quality brass India makes.

JAPAN LUSTER

The luster glaze was made to resemble copper, silver or gold. It has been used since the sixteenth century. Most of the luster ware found today was made during the nineteenth century. Japan used the luster glaze from 1920 through 1941, and made many beautiful wall pockets during this period.

ROW 1:

1. Gold luster with colorful bird and white blossoms, marked with a red ink stamp "MADE IN JAPAN".   **$30 - 40**

2. Luster, partial gold with multicolored flowers, marked with a red ink stamp "MADE IN JAPAN".   **$40 - 50**

3. Gold luster with colorful birds and white blossoms, marked with a red ink stamp "MADE IN JAPAN".   **$30 - 40**

ROW 2:

1. Gold luster with dragon, marked in a black ink stamp "HAND PAINTED MADE IN JAPAN".   **$40 - 50**

2. Gold and blue luster with colorful bird and blossoms, marked with a red ink stamp "HAND-PAINTED JAPAN".   **$40 - 50**

3. Orange and white luster with bird and pink blossoms, marked with a black ink stamp "MADE IN JAPAN".   **$30 - 40**

ROW 3:

1. Gold luster with multi colored flowers, marked with a red ink stamp "HAND-PAINTED MADE IN JAPAN".   **$30 - 40**

2. Partial gold luster with Dutch windmill and trees, marked with a gold ink stamp "MADE IN JAPAN".   **$40 - 50**

3. Gold luster with colorful bird and white and pink blossoms, marked with a red ink stamp "MADE IN JAPAN".   **$40 - 50**

Japan Luster

ROW 1:

1. Blue luster with a green bird and white blossoms, marked with a red ink stamp "MADE IN JAPAN".   **$35 - 40**

2. Blue luster with bird and white blossoms, marked with a red ink stamp 'MADE IN JAPAN".   **$40 - 50**

3. Blue luster with red flowers, marked with a red ink stamp 'HAND-PAINTED MADE IN JAPAN".   **$30 - 40**

ROW 2:

1. Blue luster with a red bird and white blossoms, marked with a green ink stamp "HAND-PAINTED MADE IN JAPAN".   **$40 - 50**

2. Partial luster, tan bird sitting on a limb, marked with a red ink stamp "HAND PAINTED MADE IN JAPAN".   **$45 - 55**

3. Blue luster with two colorful birds, marked with a green ink stamp "MADE IN JAPAN".   **$50 - 60**

ROW 3:

1. Luster with multicolored flowers, marked with a red ink stamp 'MADE IN JAPAN".   **$40 - 50**

2. Blue luster with yellow butterfly sitting on an orange poppy flower, marked with a red ink stamp "HAND-PAINTED MADE IN JAPAN".   **$40 - 50**

3. Blue luster with blue and yellow butterfly, marked with a black ink stamp "HAND-PAINTED TRICO NAGOYA-JAPAN".   **$40 - 50**

Japan Luster

ROW 1:

    1. White and blue luster with red and yellow flower, marked with a black ink stamp "HAND-PAINTED MADE IN JAPAN".   **$30 - 35**

    2. White and pearl luster with colorful bird and multicolored flowers, marked with red ink stamp "HAND-PAINTED JAPAN".   **$40 - 50**

    3. White and gold luster with BETTY BOOP and her dog, marked with red ink stamp "BETTY BOOP DES. L COPP BY FLEISCHER STUDIOS MADE IN JAPAN".   **$100 - 125**

ROW 2:

    1. Luster Cuckoo Clock, time is 9:00 o'clock, marked with a red ink stamp "M-MADE IN JAPAN", and also impressed "JAPAN".   **$20 - 25**

    2. White and gold luster with red and blue flowers, marked with a black ink stamp "MADE IN JAPAN".   **$35 - 40**

    3. Luster with colorful peacock, mark incised "MADE IN JAPAN."   **$35 - 40**

ROW 3:

    1. Pearl and green luster with red and pink flowers, marked with a green ink stamp "MADE IN JAPAN".   **$40 - 50**

    2. White with blue luster with an oriental scene, marked with a red ink stamp "GOLD CASTLE HAND-PAINTED CHIKUSA MADE IN JAPAN".   **$40 - 50**

    3. Pearl and blue luster with blue bird and multicolored flowers, marked with a black ink stamp "HAND-PAINTED MADE IN JAPAN."   **$40 - 50**

ROW 4:

    White and gold luster with multicolored flowers. Marked with a red ink stamp "MADE IN JAPAN".   **$25 - 35 ea.**

Japan Luster

ROW 1:

1. Gold and blue luster, bird sitting on a limb with blossoms, marked with a red ink stamp "HAND-PAINTED JAPAN".   **$40 - 55**

2. Blue luster with red bird on a tree limb, marked in red ink stamp "HAND-PAINTED JAPAN".   **$45 - 60**

3. Gold and blue luster with flying bird, marked with a red ink stamp "HAND-PAINTED JAPAN".   **$40 - 55**

ROW 2:

1. Gold and blue luster with colorful flying duck, marked with a red ink stamp "HAND-PAINTED MADE IN JAPAN".   **$40 - 55**

2. Red and white luster with long tailed bird sitting on limb, marked with a red ink stamp "HAND-PAINTED JAPAN".   **$40 - 55**

3. Multicolored luster with pagoda and country scene, marked with a green ink stamp "HAND-PAINTED MADE IN JAPAN".   **$45 - 55**

ROW 3:

1. Blue and gold luster with colorful flying duck, marked with a red ink stamp "HAND-PAINTED JAPAN".   **$40 - 55**

2. Pearl and gold luster with two colorful flying ducks, marked with a red ink stamp "HAND-PAINTED JAPAN".   **$40 - 55**

3. Light blue grey luster with colorful flying duck, marked with a red ink stamp "HAND-PAINTED JAPAN".   **$40 - 55**

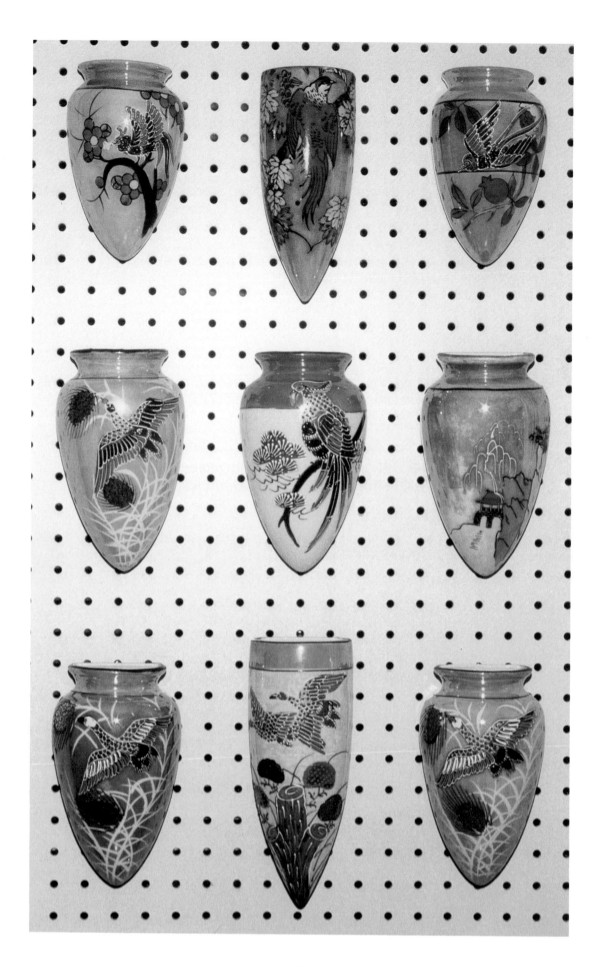

Japan Luster

ROW 1:

    1. White with pearl grey luster and red flowers, marked with a red ink stamp "MADE IN JAPAN". **$35 - 40**

    2. Red and blue luster with white flowers, marked with a red ink stamp "HAND-PAINTED MADE IN JAPAN". **$45 - 55**

    3. Multicolored luster with colorful bird, marked in a red ink stamp "HAND-PAINTED MADE IN JAPAN". **$25 - 35**

ROW 2:

    1. Blue and gold luster with small bird on limb and white blossoms, marked with a black ink stamp "MADE IN JAPAN". **$40 - 50**

    2. White and gold luster with large bird and multicolored flowers, marked with a red ink stamp "HAND-PAINTED JAPAN". **$45 - 60**

    3. White, gold and pearl grey luster with flying bird, marked with a red ink stamp "HAND-PAINTED JAPAN". **$40 - 50**

ROW 3:

    1. Multicolored luster with butterfly and flowers, marked with a red ink stamp "T-T HAND-PAINTED MADE IN JAPAN". This piece has handles. **$40 - 50**

    2. White and green luster with bird and cherries, marked with a red ink stamp "HAND-PAINTED MADE IN JAPAN". **$45 - 55**

    3. Gold luster with butterfly and red flower, marked "T-T HAND-PAINTED MADE IN JAPAN". This piece has handles and an ornate design on the bottom, **$45 - 55**

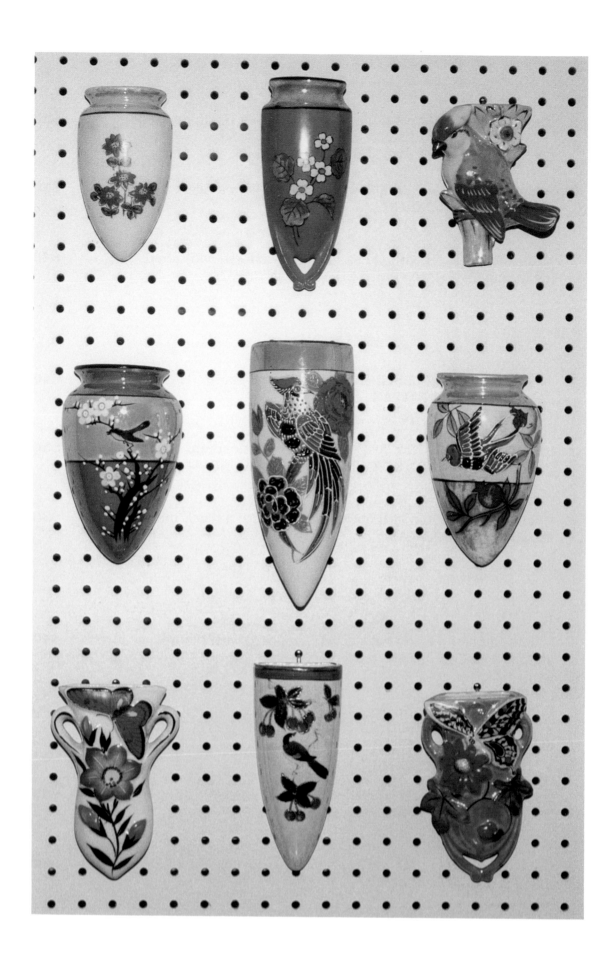

Japan Luster

ROW 1:

1. Blue and gold luster with bird, marked with a red ink stamp "HAND-PAINTED JAPAN". **$50 - 60**

2. White and red luster with flowers, marked with a black ink stamp "MADE IN JAPAN". **$50 - 60**

3. Multicolored luster with old sailing ship, marked with a red ink stamp "T-T HAND-PAINTED MADE IN JAPAN". **$40 - 50**

ROW 2:

1. Gold luster with bird, marked with a red ink stamp "HAND-PAINTED MADE IN JAPAN". **$40 - 50**

2. Red luster with flowers, marked with a red ink stamp "GOLD CASTLE HAND-PAINTED CHIKUSA MADE IN JAPAN". **$50 - 60**

3. Gold and blue luster with flower, marked with a black ink stamp "MADE IN JAPAN". **$30 - 40**

ROW 3:

1. Yellow and white luster with flowers, marked with red ink stamp "MADE IN JAPAN". **$40 - 50**

2. White and pearl grey luster with floral design, marked with a black ink stamp "GOLD CASTLE HAND-PAINTED CHIKUSA MADE IN JAPAN". **$50 - 60**

3. Gold and blue luster with bird, marked in a red ink stamp "HAND-PAINTED JAPAN". **$40 - 50**

4. Gold luster with a bird and blossoms, marked with a black ink stamp "MADE IN JAPAN". **$50 - 60**

Japan Luster

ROW 1:

    1. Gold, red and blue luster, marked with a red ink stamp "MADE IN JAPAN".   **$40 - 50**

    2. Yellow and white luster with flowers, marked with a red ink stamp "HAND-PAINTED JAPAN".   **$40 - 50**

    3. Gold luster with flowers, marked with a black ink stamp "MADE IN JAPAN".   **$40 - 50**

    4. White and blue luster with bird, marked with a black ink stamp "MADE IN JAPAN".   **$50 - 60**

ROW 2:

    1. Gold and blue luster, plain, marked with a black ink stamp "HAND-PAINTED JAPAN".   **$35 - 40**

    2. Gold and blue luster geese, marked with a black ink stamp "MADE IN JAPAN".   **$60 - 75**

    3. Blue and gold luster with bird, marked with a red ink stamp "JAPAN".   **$40 - 50**

ROW 3:

    1. Red luster with flowers, marked with a green ink stamp "HAND-PAINTED MADE IN JAPAN".   **$40 - 50**

    2. Yellow and blue luster with flowers, marked with a red ink stamp "HAND-PAINTED JAPAN".   **$40 - 50**

    3. Blue and yellow luster with bird, marked with a red ink stamp "HAND-PAINTED JAPAN".   **$40 - 50**

    4. White and grey luster with flower, marked with a green ink stamp "HAND-PAINTED MADE IN JAPAN".   **$25 - 30**

ROW 4:

    1. Gold and blue luster with ferns, marked with a red ink stamp "MADE IN JAPAN".   **$35 - 45**

    2. Plain blue luster, marked with a paper label "MADE IN JAPAN".   **$35 - 45**

    3. White with red and blue luster, marked with a black ink stamp "MADE IN JAPAN".   **$35 - 45**

    4. Gold and blue luster with flowers, marked with a black ink stamp "MADE IN JAPAN".   **$35 - 45**

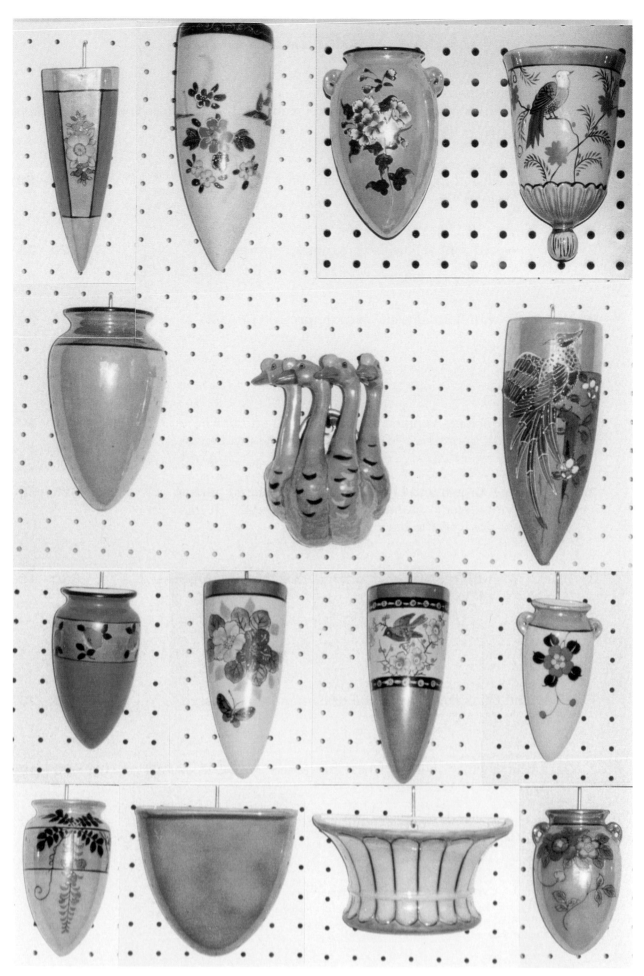

JAPAN MISCELLANEOUS

The Japan miscellaneous section is made up of the many different types of wall pockets made by Japan other than Nippon, Noritake, Luster and Occupied Japan. These wall pockets are very easy to find and can still be bought at a reasonable price.

ROW 1:

    1. Indian Chief, soft matte brown finish, mark impressed "MADE IN JAPAN".   **$50 - 60**

    2. Brown colored with yellow flowers, mark impressed "MADE IN JAPAN".   **$20 - 25**

    3. Blue color with floral design, mark impressed "MADE IN JAPAN".   **$15 - 20**

ROW 2:

    1. Basket type, black trimmed with red, a bird and flower design, mark impressed "MADE IN JAPAN", (extra heavy).   **$40 - 50**

    2. Basket type, brown and blue with a bright colored parrot, marked with a black ink stamp "MADE IN JAPAN". It has an original price on the back 25¢.   **$25 - 30**

    3. Black color with red and gold, oriental design, mark impressed "MADE IN JAPAN", (extra heavy).   **$30 - 40**

ROW 3:

    1. Silver and black color with floral design, mark impressed "MADE IN JAPAN".   **$15 - 20**

    2. Dark brown with two frogs, mark impressed "MADE IN JAPAN".   **$30 - 40**

    3. Old gold color, with two dragonflies and thistle design, mark incised "MADE IN JAPAN".   **$15 - 20**

Japan Miscellaneous

ROW 1:

    1. Orange color with multicolored flowers and leaves, marked   **$25 - 30**
with a red ink stamp "The Hirode JAPAN".

    2. Aqua blue with yellow and mauve colored flowers, marked with   **$35 - 40**
a black ink stamp "MADE IN JAPAN".

    3. Blue and pink colored with two white cherubs, mark   **$25 - 30**
impressed "MADE IN JAPAN".

ROW 2:

    1. Mauve and yellow color with a pineapple design, marked with   **$20 - 30**
a black ink stamp "MADE IN JAPAN".

    2. Large blue wall pocket with white and yellow daisy flowers,   **$40 - 50**
mark impressed "MADE IN JAPAN".

    3. Mauve and yellow color with pineapple design, marked with
black in stamp "MADE IN JAPAN".

    Price per pair – **$40 - 60**

ROW 3:

    1. Green basket pattern with red and yellow flowers, marked   **$20 - 25**
with a black ink stamp "MADE IN JAPAN".

    2. Orange to yellow color with yellow flowers, marked with a   **$30 - 40**
red ink stamp "HAND PAINTED TRICO NAGOYA JAPAN".

    3. Green reeds with yellow swan sitting in water, marked with a   **$25 - 35**
black ink stamp "MADE IN JAPAN", and it also has an impressed
mark "MADE IN JAPAN".

Japan Miscellaneous

ROW 1:

   1. Tan with a yellow bird and blue wings with blue flowers, marked with a black ink stamp "MADE IN JAPAN".   **$15 - 20**

   2. Green basket with red handles and flowers, marked with a black ink stamp "MADE IN JAPAN". It also has an impressed mark "MADE IN JAPAN", and has an original price on back $1.00.   **$40 - 50**

   3. Tan with two birds and mauve colored flowers, marked with black ink stamp "MADE IN JAPAN".   **$15 - 20**

ROW 2:

   1. Purple color with handles and multicolored flowers, marked with black ink stamp "MADE IN JAPAN".   **$30 - 35**

   2. Green basket pattern with bright multicolored flowers, mark impressed "MADE IN JAPAN".   **$30 - 40**

   3. Purple color with floral design, mark incised "MADE IN JAPAN".   **$25 - 30**

ROW 3:

   1. Tan colored pitcher with brown handles and a fancy yellow bird, marked with a black ink stamp "MADE IN JAPAN".   **$20 - 25**

   2. Green basket pattern with handles and multicolored flowers, marked with a black ink stamp "MADE IN JAPAN".   **$30 - 40**

   3. Tan color with handles and colorful fruit, marked with a black ink stamp "A" and "MADE IN JAPAN".   **$20 - 25**

113

Japan Miscellaneous

ROW 1:

1. Black colored pocket with red flower design, mark impressed "MADE IN JAPAN".   **$15 - 20**

2. Black pocket with blue and red bird design, mark impressed "MADE IN JAPAN".   **$15 - 20**

3. Black pocket, extra small, with red rose design, mark impressed "MADE IN JAPAN".   **$15 - 20**

4. Black pocket multicolored floral design, mark impressed "MADE IN JAPAN".   **$15 - 20**

5. Black pocket with blue, yellow and red design, mark impressed "MADE IN JAPAN".   **$15 - 20**

ROW 2:

1. Black and grey pocket trimmed in red with silver leaf, has a bird and floral design, marked twice, impressed "MADE IN JAPAN".   **$30 - 35**

2. Large black with brown leaves and red berries with gold accents, mark impressed "MADE IN JAPAN".   **$40 - 45**

3. Black with multicolored red bird on a tree limb, mark impressed "MADE IN JAPAN".   **$25 - 30**

ROW 3:

1. Green and tan color pocket with a bird and floral design, no markings. This piece does not have the same finish as the other pieces on this page, it has a dark green glaze inside. The top border design is the same as Japan wall pockets.   **$40 - 50**

2. Green and blue pocket with multicolored red bird, mark impressed "MADE IN JAPAN".   **$25 - 30**

3. Green and blue colored pocket, same design as #2 above, only smaller.   **$20 - 25**

NOTE:

The finish on the wall pockets on this page are supposed to simulate tree bark cloisonne over a porcelain body. They were shown in a Spring 1928 Sears catalog under the brand name TOKANABE and sold for 79¢ each.

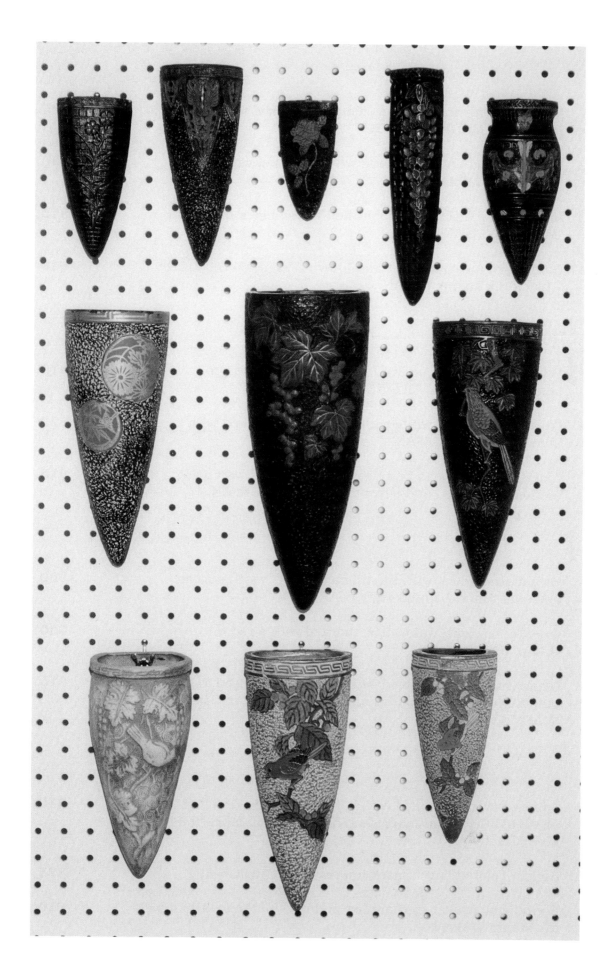

115

Japan Miscellaneous

ROW 1:

1. Madonna with stained glass window, marked with a black ink stamp "MADE IN JAPAN".   **$25 - 30**

2. Madonna and child, blue and white, marked with a red ink stamp "JAPAN".   **$30 - 35**

3. Angel with purple flowers, marked with a black ink stamp "MADE IN JAPAN".   **$15 - 20**

4. Blue vase type with green and brown design, marked with a black ink stamp "JAPAN".   **$10 - 15**

ROW 2:

1. Brown clock with a squirrel, marked with a silver foil label "Hand-painted TILSO JAPAN".   **$15 - 20**

2. Lavabo, green and white with gold spout, marked with a blue paper label "JAPAN".   **$20 - 25**

3. Clock with deer head and two birds, trimmed with gold, marked with a red and silver foil label "PAC JAPAN".   **$15 - 20**

ROW 3:

1. Grandfather clock with thermometer, "74°", with a silver foil label "Hand-painted TILSO JAPAN".   **$20 - 25**

2. Oriental boy with water jugs, marked with a red ink stamp "JAPAN".   **$20 - 25**

3. Little white clock trimmed with gold, mark incised "4134 MADE IN JAPAN", and also marked with a red ink stamp "MADE IN JAPAN".   **$10 - 15**

ROW 4:

1. Square picture trimmed with gold, marked on front "MAD AS A HATTER", and marked on back on a foil label "IMPORTS ENESCO JAPAN".   **$10 - 15**

2. Copper colored bagel, mark impressed "FOREIGN 671".   **$25 - 30**

3. Round wall pocket with pitcher and pot, marked with a black ink stamp "JAPAN".   **$10 - 15**

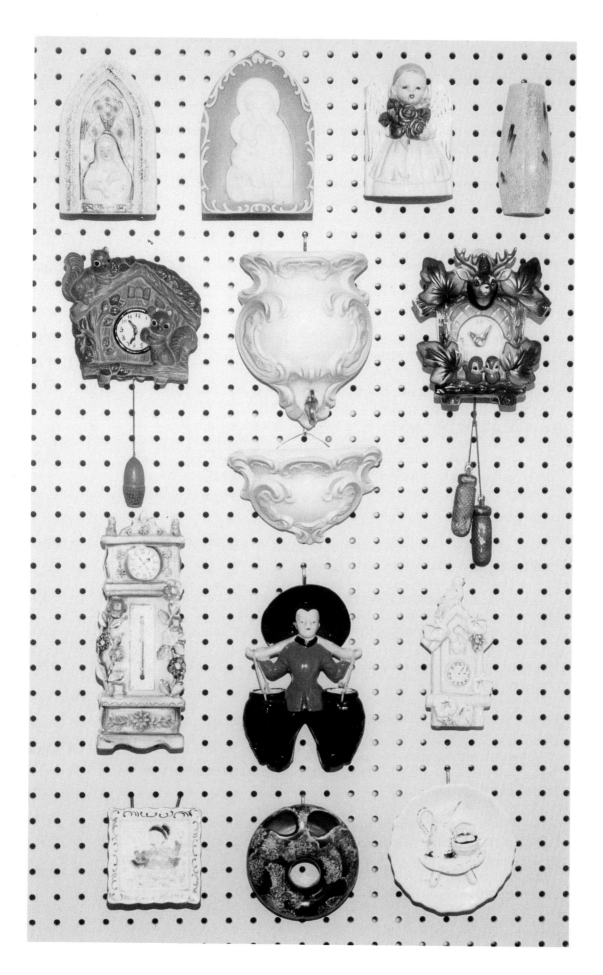

Japan Miscellaneous

ROW 1:

1. Oriental man with bamboo trim, marked with a black ink stamp "MADE IN JAPAN". **$25 - 30**

2. Vase type pocket, yellow with pink flowers, marked with a gold ink stamp "MADE IN JAPAN". **$45 - 55**

3. Oriental woman with bamboo trim, marked with a black ink stamp "MADE IN JAPAN". **$25 - 30**

Price per pair – **$60 - 70**

ROW 2:

1. Boy with dancing girl, marked with a blue ink stamp "© 1956 COPYRIGHT JAPAN L & M". **$20 - 25**

2. Violin with music book, marked with a silver foil label "HAND-PAINTED LENWILE CHINA - MADE IN JAPAN". It also has a red ink stamp that reads "NC 6869A". **$20 - 25**

3. Pair of blue baby shoes with pink flowers, marked with a black ink stamp "© N.Y. PIONEER MDSE. CO. JAPAN". **$10 - 15**

ROW 3:

1. Colorful ladies shoe with a red bow, marked with a green ink stamp "MADE IN JAPAN". **$20 - 25**

2. Ladies hat with mauve flowers, marked with a black ink stamp "© Geo. Z. Lefton 4361". It also is marked with a red foil label "LEFTON TRADE MARK EXCLUSIVES JAPAN". **$40 - 50**

3. Ladies shoe with black heel, marked with a green ink stamp "MADE IN JAPAN". **$20 - 25**

ROW 4:

1. Ladies hat with green and pink trim, marked with a blue ink stamp "MADE IN JAPAN". An original J. J. NEWBERRY CO. price tag 98¢. **$30 - 40**

2. Small ladies hat, marked with a black ink stamp "MADE IN JAPAN (T) PATENT NO. 84066". **$10 - 15**

3. Ladies hat, marked with a blue ink stamp "MADE IN JAPAN". An original J. J. NEWBERRY CO. price tag 98¢. (Same as #1). **$30 - 40**

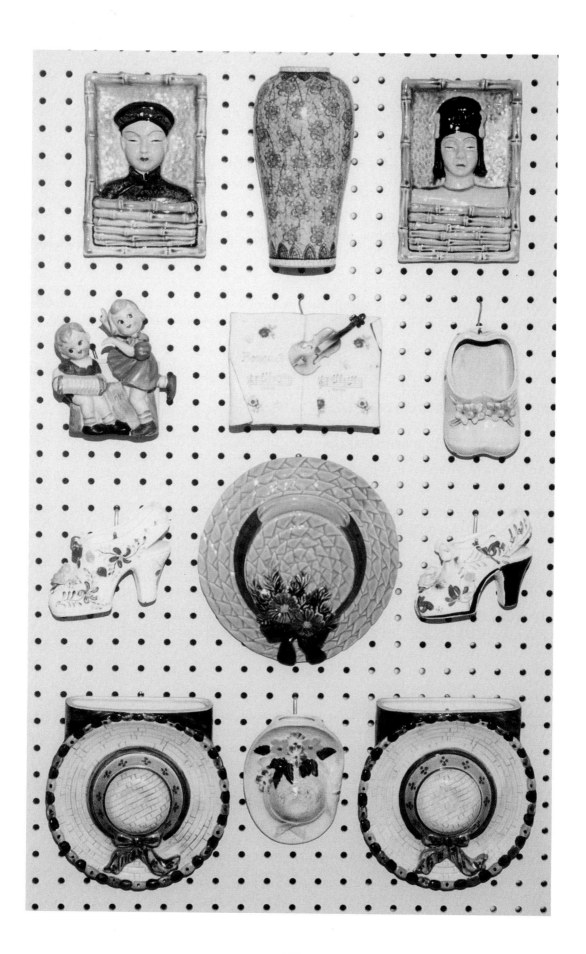

119

Japan Miscellaneous

ROW 1:

1. Yellow and blue bird on a pitcher, gold trim, marked with black and silver foil label "WALES MADE IN JAPAN". **$30 - 35**

2. Two yellow birds in a bird house, marked with a brown ink stamp "© Japan". **$20 - 25**

3. Blue and brown bird on pitcher, gold trim, marked with a black and silver foil label "WALES MADE IN JAPAN". **$30 - 35**

ROW 2:

1. Oriole bird and berries on limb, marked with a paper label "Supreme Ware T.M.C. JAPAN". It also has a black ink stamp "ORIOLE". **$20 - 25**

2. Waxwing bird with leaves and berries, marked with purple ink stamp "WAXWING", also marked with a silver foil label "Hand-painted THAMES MADE IN JAPAN". **$30 - 35**

3. Colorful peacock, marked with a blue ink stamp "MADE IN JAPAN". **$25 - 30**

ROW 3:

1. Red Cardinal bird and flowers, marked with a silver and red foil label "Ucagco CERAMICS JAPAN". **$15 - 20**

2. Red Cardinal bird and pink flower, marked with a green ink stamp "CARDINAL JAPAN". **$15 - 20**

3. Red Cardinal bird, marked with a silver and red foil label "Ucagco CERAMICS JAPAN". (This is part of an opposite pair).
Price per pair – **$35 - 45**

ROW 4:

1. Blue Jay bird and flowers, marked with a silver and red foil label "Ucagco CERAMICS JAPAN". **$15 - 20**

2. Yellow bird and apple with gold, marked with a red foil label "Original Dee Bee Co., Import HAND-PAINTED JAPAN". **$15 - 20**

3. Blue Jay bird, marked with a silver and red foil label "Ucagco CERAMICS JAPAN". (This is part of an opposite pair).
Price per pair – **$35 - 45**

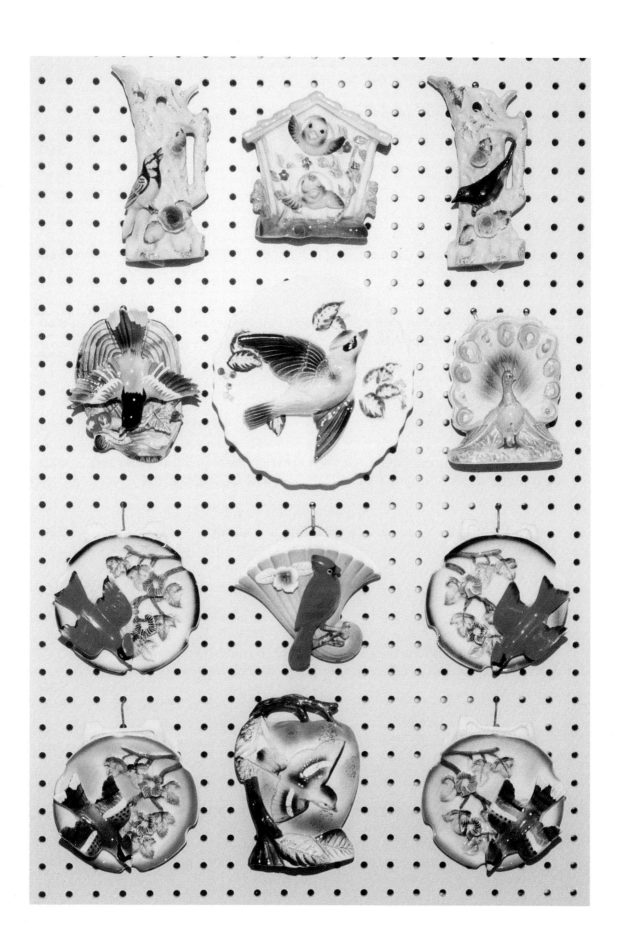

Japan Miscellaneous

ROW 1:

    1. Two small colorful Chinese ring neck rooster pheasants, marked with black ink stamp "JAPAN".

Price each – $10 - 15

ROW 2:

    1. Medium size colorful Chinese ring neck rooster pheasant, marked with a black ink stamp "JAPAN".   **$15 - 20**

    2. Large colorful Chinese ring neck rooster pheasant, marked with a black ink stamp "JAPAN".   **$20 - 25**

Price per set – $50 - 65

ROW 3:

    1. Flying green head mallard duck with crescent background, marked with a green ink stamp "TORH BRAND MADE IN JAPAN".   **$25 - 30**

    2. Colorful flying duck, marked with a blue ink stamp "MADE IN JAPAN".   **$15 - 20**

ROW 4:

Pair of flying green head mallard ducks with plate background, both are marked with a blue paper label "MADE IN JAPAN".

Price each – $30 - 35
Price per set – $60 - 70

ROW 5:

Set of three white swans, consisting of one large and two small. Marked with a blue paper label "MADE IN JAPAN". The large swan is a wall pocket, the two small ones are not.

Price per set of three – $25 - 30

Japan Miscellaneous

ROW 1:

1. Blue bird sitting on fruit, marked on a paper label "MADE IN JAPAN". $20 - 25

2. Cuckoo clock, multicolored brown to green, marked with a black ink stamp "P-421", and also has a paper label "REG. US. PAT. OFF. NORCREST JAPAN". $20 - 25

3. Small wall pocket with a deer head, marked with a black ink stamp "JAPAN". $15 - 20

ROW 2:

1. Holy water font with angel, gold trim, mark incised "JAPAN". $25 - 30

2. Multicolored bird on a tree trunk, marked with a black ink stamp "MADE IN JAPAN". $25 - 30

ROW 3:

1. Multicolored bird on tree trunk, mark impressed "MADE IN JAPAN". $30 - 35

2. Luster, pearl colored with red top, marked with a red ink stamp "GOLD CASTLE HAND-PAINTED CHIKUSA MADE IN JAPAN". $40 - 50

3. Yellow lily, (this wall pocket looks a lot like the Abingdon lily, it is not as wide or as heavy as the Abingdon). It is plainly marked in a black ink stamp "MADE IN JAPAN". $30 - 35

ROW 4:

1. Double cone with bright multicolored flowers, marked with a black ink stamp "K-FLOWER JAPAN". $20 - 30

2. Bright multicolored bird with red berries, marked with a black ink stamp "MADE IN JAPAN". $40 - 50

3. Cute little face in a peace lily, marked with a green ink stamp "PY-NC JAPAN". $20 - 25

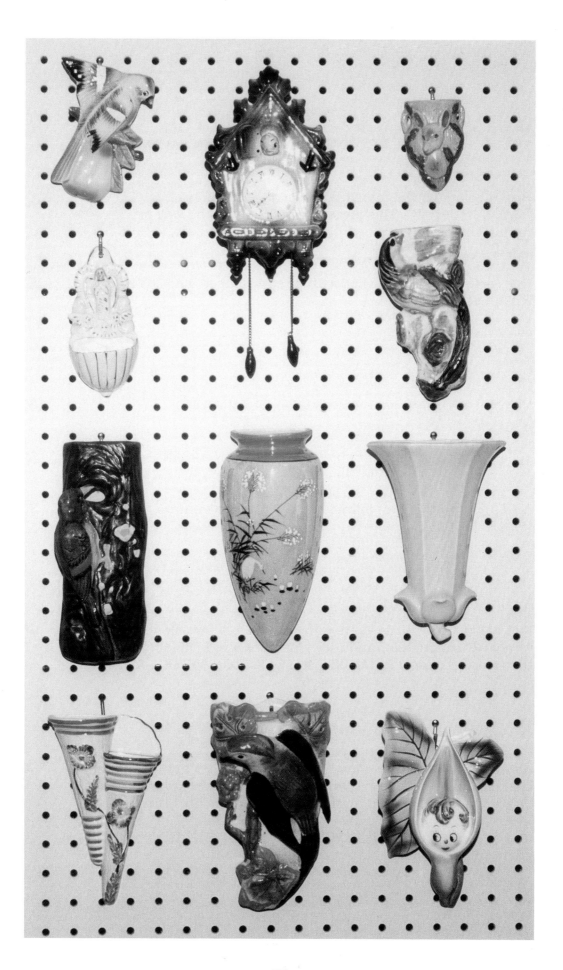

Japan Miscellaneous

ROW 1:

1. Owl, new clay type, marked with a gold foil label "SAN $10 - 15
   FRANCISCO 94103 ® COUNTERPOINT MADE IN JAPAN".

2. Bright colored owl sitting in a crescent, mark impressed $40 - 50
   "MADE IN JAPAN". This piece can be hung on the wall or
   from a chain.

3. Owl, new clay type, marked with a red foil label "NAPCoWARE $10 - 15
   N IMPORT JAPAN".

ROW 2:

1. Colorful owl, mark impressed "MADE IN JAPAN". $20 - 30

2. Yellow frog on leaf, mark impressed "MADE IN JAPAN". $20 - 25

3. Bird and strawberries, marked with a black ink stamp $30 - 40
   "MADE IN JAPAN".

ROW 3:

Pair of cute little birds, both marked with a green ink stamp $50 - 75
"© geo. Z. Lefton 283", and they also have a red foil label
that reads "Lefton's REG. U.S. PAT. OFF. EXCLUSIVES JAPAN".

ROW 4:

A pair of beautiful little blond girls all dressed up in blue, holding $60 - 80
baskets, both are marked with a green ink stamp "© geo. Z. Lefton
1956 - 50264". It also is marked with a red foil label that reads
"Lefton's REG. U.S. PAT. OFF. EXCLUSIVES JAPAN". This is a
true opposite pair, made in 1956. There is a set of these, with
a boy and girl holding baskets made by Lefton.

127

Japan Miscellaneous

ROW 1:

1. A colorful bird with a long beak and purple berries, marked with a black ink stamp "MADE IN JAPAN", (made of clay). **$25 - 30**

2. A colorful bird with a long beak and orange berries, marked with a red ink stamp "HAND-PAINTED MADE IN JAPAN". This wall pocket is 1/2" shorter than #1 bird and made of porcelain. **$30 - 35**

3. A colorful parrot with a red cornucopia. The mark is impressed "MADE IN JAPAN". (This piece is made to hang on a wall or hang from a chain. **$25 - 30**

4. Red crested bird, marked with a black ink stamp "MADE IN JAPAN". **$25 - 30**

ROW 2:

1. Colorful bird sitting on a basket, marked with a black ink stamp "MADE IN JAPAN". **$50 - 60**

2. A bird with multicolored flowers. The mark is impressed "MADE IN JAPAN". **$30 - 35**

3. Two birds with long tails, mark impressed "MADE IN JAPAN". This pocket has the original selling price on back of $1.00. **$40 - 50**

ROW 3:

1. Parrot with a green head, mark impressed "M-MADE IN JAPAN". This has the original selling price on back of 25¢. **$40 - 50**

2. Red and yellow bird sitting on a black tree limb, (accented with gold), mark incised with oriental letters, also marked with a red ink stamp "MADE IN JAPAN". **$35 - 40**

3. Colorful parrot with blue head, mark impressed "MADE IN JAPAN". **$40 - 50**

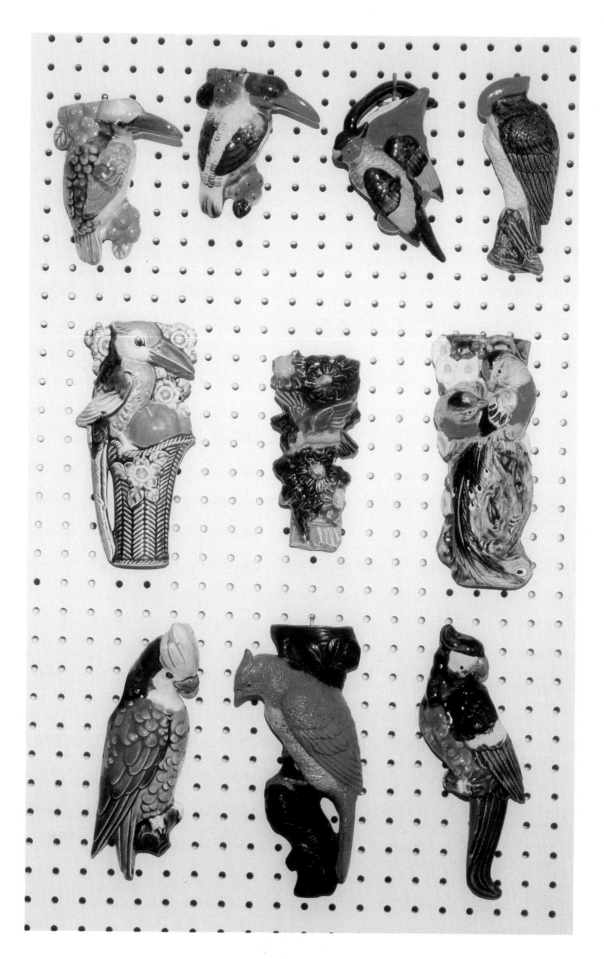

Japan Miscellaneous

ROW 1:

Pair of yellow and brown birds, both are marked with a green ink stamp "3998", and a red foil label "Lefton's REG. U.S. PAT. OFF. EXCLUSIVES JAPAN". Written on the back of each one in pencil is "year 1967 - $3.49 ea.".

$65 - 75

ROW 2:

Pair of colorful birds on a square background, marked with a black ink stamp "MADE IN JAPAN". This pair was made to hang on a wall or stand on a table like a vase.

$65 - 80

ROW 3:

1. Yellow and red bird sitting on a green tree limb, marked with a black ink stamp "HAND-PAINTED MADE IN JAPAN".

$35 - 40

2. Yellow and blue parrot sitting on a limb, mark impressed "MADE IN JAPAN".

$35 - 40

3. Colorful parrot sitting on a limb, mark impressed "MADE IN JAPAN".

$35 - 40

ROW 4:

1. Parakeet and yellow flowers on a blue vase, mark impressed "MADE IN JAPAN".

$60 - 80

2. Colorful parrot sitting on a brown tree limb, mark impressed "MADE IN JAPAN".

$50 - 60

3. A large mauve and yellow parrot sitting on a blue limb, mark impressed "MADE IN JAPAN". This piece is extra heavy and the mold marks are different. Extra nice wall pocket. *Marvin calls this "SUPER BIRD"*.

$60 - 80

Japan Miscellaneous

ROW 1:

1. Orange and white hanging moon planter, marked with a black ink stamp "M-HAND-PAINTED JAPAN".   **$35 - 40**

2. Red hanging moon planter with flying geese , marked with a black ink stamp "MADE IN JAPAN".   **$35 - 40**

ROW 2:

A colorful macaw bird, mark impressed "MADE IN JAPAN". This piece originally had a metal hanger that the macaw sat in.   **$25 - 30**

ROW 3:

1. A blue hanging moon planter with an Oriental woman, mark impressed "MADE IN JAPAN".   **$35 - 40**

2. Colorful parrot with multicolored flowers on a hanging moon planter, mark impressed "MADE IN JAPAN".   **$45 - 50**

ROW 4:

Porcelain chain with two hooks and a ring for hanging the moon planters or the parrots. These chains are usually missing when you find the moon or parrot planters. They probably got broken or misplaced over the years.   **$25 - 30**

ROW 5:

1. A pair of colorful parrots sitting together on a tree limb, marked with a black ink stamp "MADE IN JAPAN". (The porcelain chain was missing).   **$40 - 50**

2. A colorful parrot sitting on a tree limb, marked with a black ink stamp "MADE IN JAPAN". (The porcelain chain was missing).   **$35 - 40**

3. A pair of colorful parrots sitting together on a tree limb, (different color than #1 pair) marked with a black ink stamp "MADE IN JAPAN". (The porcelain chain was missing).   **$40 - 50**

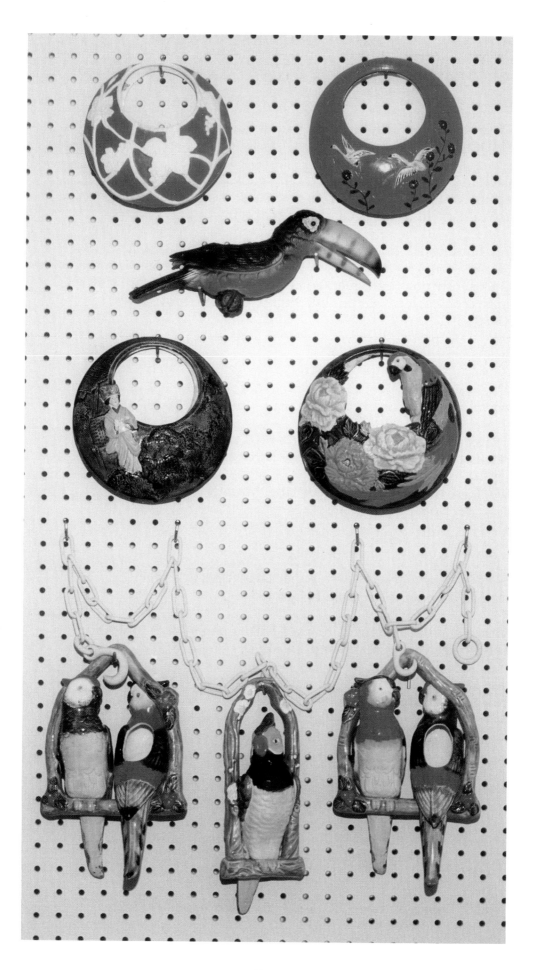

133

Japan Miscellaneous

ROW 1:

    1. White scotty dog head, marked with a black ink stamp "MADE IN JAPAN".   **$45 - 50**

    2. Black mule weather forecaster, marked with a black ink stamp "MADE IN JAPAN". This piece is shown again with instructions in the miscellaneous chapter.   **$20 - 25**

    3. Tiny horse head, marked with a black ink stamp "JAPAN".   **$10 - 15**

    4. Black scotty dog head, marked on front "WISCONSIN DELLS". Marked on back with a red ink stamp "JAPAN", and incised "KKS536".   **$30 - 35**

ROW2:

    1. Brown boxer dog head, marked with blue paper label "JAPAN".   **$25 - 30**

    2. Kittens, bugs and strawberries, marked with a silver foil label "HAND-PAINTED PICO JAPAN".   **$25 - 30**

    3. Two dogs, marked with a paper label "JAPAN".   **$15 - 20**

ROW 3:

    1. Yellow kitten, marked with a paper label "JAPAN". The original price on the bottom is 59¢.   **$10 - 15**

    2. Mother and baby squirrel, marked with a paper label "JAPAN". It also has a brown ink stamp "C-7594".   **$25 - 30**

    3. Blue kitten, marked with paper label "JAPAN". The original price is on the back 59¢.   **$10 - 15**

ROW 4:

    1. Kitten with green hat, marked with a black ink stamp "MADE IN JAPAN".   **$15 - 20**

    2. Elephant head, marked with a green ink stamp "JAPAN", also marked with a black and silver foil label "Dickson MADE IN JAPAN".   **$15 - 20**

    3. Pig with broom and bee, marked with paper label "JAPAN".   **$15 - 20**

135

Japan Miscellaneous

ROW 1:

1. Tea kettle with rooster design, marked with a silver foil label "A Napco Ceramic JAPAN", also marked with a green ink stamp "S727R".   **$10 - 15**

2. Teapot with rooster design, marked the same as #1.   **$10 - 15**

3. Water sprinkler with rooster design, marked the same as #1.   **$10 - 15**

ROW 2:

1. Pitcher and bowl, marked with silver foil label "Ucagco CERAMICS JAPAN".   **$20 - 25**

2. Funnel, marked with a silver foil label "JAPAN" and also marked with a green ink stamp "© HAND DECORATED".   **$10 - 15**

3. Water sprinkler, marked with black ink stamp "P337", and also marked with a blue foil label "REG. U.S. PAT. OFF. NORCREST JAPAN".   **$10 - 15**

ROW 3:

1. Rolling pin, marked with a black ink stamp "P104", and also marked with a blue foil label "REG. U.S. PAT. OFF. NORCREST JAPAN".   **$10 - 15**

2. Dust pan, marked with a black ink stamp "7012", and also red foil label "MADE IN JAPAN".   **$3 - 5**

ROW 4:

1. Skillet that reads "OUR HOUSE IS ALWAYS OPEN TO SUNSHINE FRIENDS AND GUEST". Marked with a blue foil label "REG. U.S. PAT. OFF. NORCREST JAPAN".   **$10 - 15**

2. Skillet with yellow handle that reads "TOO MANY COOKS SPOIL THE BROTH" and a silver foil label marked "JAPAN".   **$10 - 15**

3. Skillet with "kitchen prayer", marked with blue foil label "REG. U.S. PAT. OFF. NORCREST JAPAN". Handwritten on back "MOM AUG. 29 1967".   **$10 - 15**

Japan Miscellaneous

ROW 1:

1. Smiley corn, marked with a green ink stamp "Hand-painted MADE IN JAPAN". **$25 - 30**

2. Basket full of fruit, mark impressed "MADE IN JAPAN". **$30 - 40**

3. Yellow pears, marked with a black ink stamp "MADE IN JAPAN". **$20 - 25**

ROW 2:

1. Yellow pear with wire holder, marked with a red foil label "LIPPER & MANN CREATIONS JAPAN". **$25 - 30**

2. Lavabo with fruit design (two pieces), marked with a blue foil label "ORIGINAL ARNART-CREATION", and also marked with a black ink stamp "Capri by Arnart 33/257". **$25 - 30**

3. Yellow pear with wire holder, marked same as #1.   Price per pair – **$50 - 60**

ROW 3:

1. Red apples trimmed with gold, marked with paper label "JAPAN". **$15 - 20**

2. Carrots and green beans, marked with red foil label "Lefton's REG. U.S. PAT. OFF. EXCLUSIVES JAPAN", and also green ink stamp "126". **$20 - 25**

3. Strawberries, marked with black ink stamp "MADE IN JAPAN". **$15 - 20**

ROW 4:

1. Bananas, marked with a paper label "JAPAN". **$15 - 20**

2. Strawberries, marked with a green ink stamp "Hand-painted MADE IN JAPAN". **$35 - 40**

3. Peach marked with a red foil label "Lefton's REG. U.S. PAT. OFF. EXCLUSIVES JAPAN". **$15 - 20**

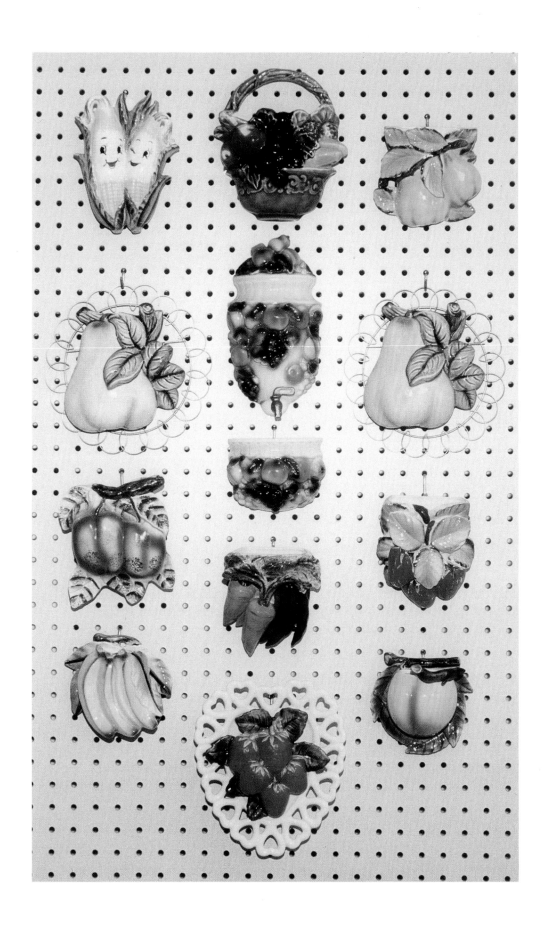

139

Japan Miscellaneous

ROW 1:

    1. Small delicate hand painted wall pocket with an oriental scene, marked with a green ink stamp "MADE IN NIPPON". (Possibly the oldest one in this book.)   **$50 - 60**

    2. Plate type with colorful country scene, marked with gold ink stamp "HAND-PAINTED UCAGCOCHINA JAPAN".   **$25 - 30**

    3. Small fish, marked with a black ink stamp "JAPAN".   **$10 - 15**

ROW 2:

    1. Small brown violin, marked with a red ink stamp "Hand-Painted ARDALT MADE IN JAPAN 6415".   **$15 - 20**

    2. Pictured frame trimmed with gold, marked with a silver foil label "Napco Ceramics JAPAN", and also a black ink stamp "K26701C".   **$25 - 30**

    3. Pink violin with flowers, marked with a red foil label "Lefton's REG. U.S. PAT. OFF. EXCLUSIVES JAPAN", and also marked with a black ink stamp "105".   **$25 - 30**

ROW 3:

    1. Violin with pink rose, trimmed with gold, marked with a black ink stamp "369", and it also has a red foil label "Lefton's REG. U.S. PAT. OFF. EXCLUSIVES JAPAN".   **$25 - 30**

    2. Man sitting in a window, marked with a black ink stamp "MADE IN JAPAN". This piece can hang on the wall or sit on a table. This may have been a comb holder.   **$40 - 50**

    3. Violin with pink rose, trimmed with gold, marked the same as #1.

Price per pair – **$50 - 60**

ROW 4:

    Violin with fruit design and green trim, marked with gold foil label and a black ink stamp "INARCO ® JAPAN E-61766".   **$20 - 25**

141

Japan Miscellaneous

ROW 1:

    1. Tulip, marked with a black ink stamp "MADE IN JAPAN".   **$25 - 30**

    2. Grapes trimmed with gold, marked with a silver foil label "BRADLEY CERAMICS JAPAN".   **$20 - 25**

    3. Cherries, mark impressed "MADE IN JAPAN".   **$25 - 30**

ROW 2:

    1. Vase type wall pocket with handles, floral design, marked with a black ink stamp "MADE IN JAPAN".   **$25 - 30**

    2. Black native in a palm tree with an alligator, marked with a blue ink stamp "MADE IN JAPAN". This piece was shown in the California chapter with the black memorabilia.   **$125 - 150**

    3. Flower and leaves, mark impressed "MADE IN JAPAN".   **$25 - 30**

ROW 3:

    1. Strawberries, mark impressed "MADE IN JAPAN".   **$25 - 30**

    2. Flowers in a basket, mark impressed "MADE IN JAPAN".   **$40 - 50**

    3. Grapes, mark impressed "MADE IN JAPAN".   **$25 - 30**

ROW 4:

    1. Tulips, marked with a black ink stamp "MADE IN JAPAN".   **$40 - 50**

    2. Lily, marked with a black ink stamp "MARUKON-K-WARE MADE IN JAPAN".   **$40 - 50**

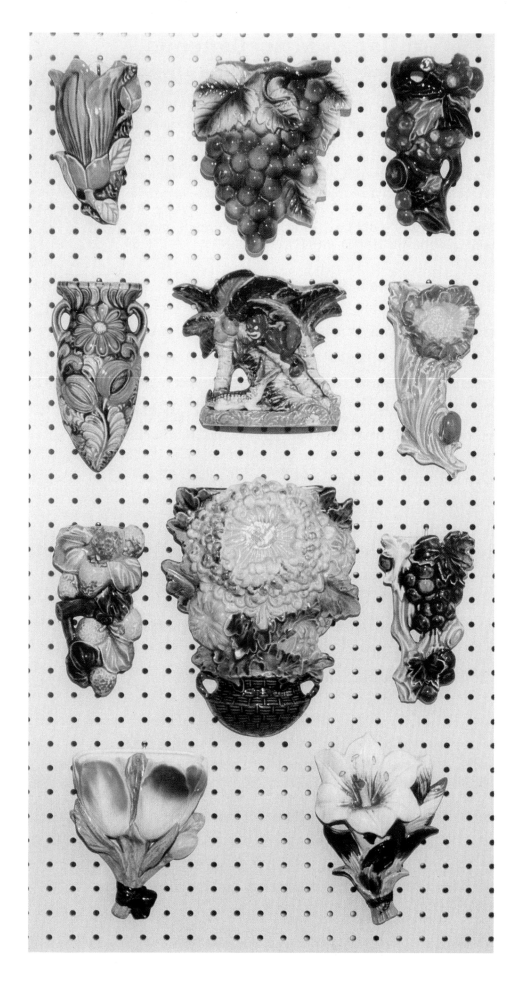

Japan Miscellaneous

ROW 1:

1. Colonial Lady with black hair and a parrot, Satsuma style finish, marked with a black ink stamp "HAND-PAINTED JAPAN".   **$60 - 75**

2. Colonial Lady with brown hair and a parrot, Satsuma style finish, marked with a red ink stamp "MADE IN JAPAN".   **$55 - 70**

3. Colonial Lady with gold fan, Satsuma style finish, marked with a black ink stamp "HAND-PAINTED JAPAN".   **$60 - 75**

ROW 2:

1. Oriental lady carrying a basket, mark impressed "MADE IN JAPAN".   **$50 - 60**

2. Colonial lady with pink rose, marked with a black ink stamp "MADE IN JAPAN". Written on the bottom of this wall pocket in pencil is "1935". This piece and the other Colonial Ladies on this page, and the next page were in a 1934 Sears and Roebuck catalog.   **$40 - 45**

3. Oriental man carrying a basket, mark impressed "MADE IN JAPAN". The man and the woman in #1 are a pair.   **$50 - 60**   Price per pair – **$110 - 125**

ROW 3:

1. Cat woman, gold accents, with real fur skirt and holding a spear. Marked with a red ink stamp "7311 JAPAN".   **$35 - 40**

2. Small vase type with handles and a dragon design. Mark impressed "MADE IN JAPAN".   **$20 - 25**

3. Cat woman without skirt and spear, no markings.   **$30 - 35**

ROW 4:

1. Satsuma style wall pocket, marked with a red ink stamp "MADE IN JAPAN".   **$40 - 50**

2. Satsuma style wall pocket with handles, marked with a black ink stamp "MADE IN JAPAN".   **$50 - 60**

3. Yellow basket weave design with berries and handles, marked "MADE IN JAPAN".   **$20 - 25**

145

Japan Miscellaneous

ROW 1:

1. Colonial lady with brown hair and parrot, gold trim and flowers, marked with a black ink stamp "MADE IN JAPAN".   **$40 - 45**

2. Colonial man playing a mandolin, gold trim and flowers, marked with a red ink stamp "HAND-PAINTED JAPAN".   **$45 - 50**

3. Colonial lady with blond hair and a fan, with gold trim and flowers, marked with a red ink stamp "HAND-PAINTED JAPAN".   **$45 - 50**

4. Colonial lady with brown hair and gold trim with flowers, marked with a red ink stamp "HAND-PAINTED JAPAN".   **$45 - 50**

ROW 2:

1. Small scotty dog, marked with a black ink stamp "JAPAN".   **$15 - 20**

2. Large scotty dog, marked with a red ink stamp "JAPAN", and also impressed "JAPAN".   **$20 - 25**

ROW3:

1. Violin with flowers, marked with a red foil label "Lefton's REG. U.S. PAT. OFF. EXCLUSIVES JAPAN", and also marked with a black ink stamp "S-814".   **$25 - 30**

2. Cornucopia with flowers, marked with a red and black ink stamp "Lefton China HAND-PAINTED".   **$25 - 30**

3. Blue vase type with red tulips, marked with a green ink stamp "MADE IN JAPAN".   **$25 - 30**

ROW 4:

1. Blue bird on apples, marked with a black ink stamp "S-7754", and it also has a paper label that reads "JAPAN".   **$20 - 25**

2. Red bird on pears, marked with a black ink stamp "S-7554", and it also has a paper label "JAPAN". This wall pocket and the one above has the same numbers and paper label.   **$20 - 25**

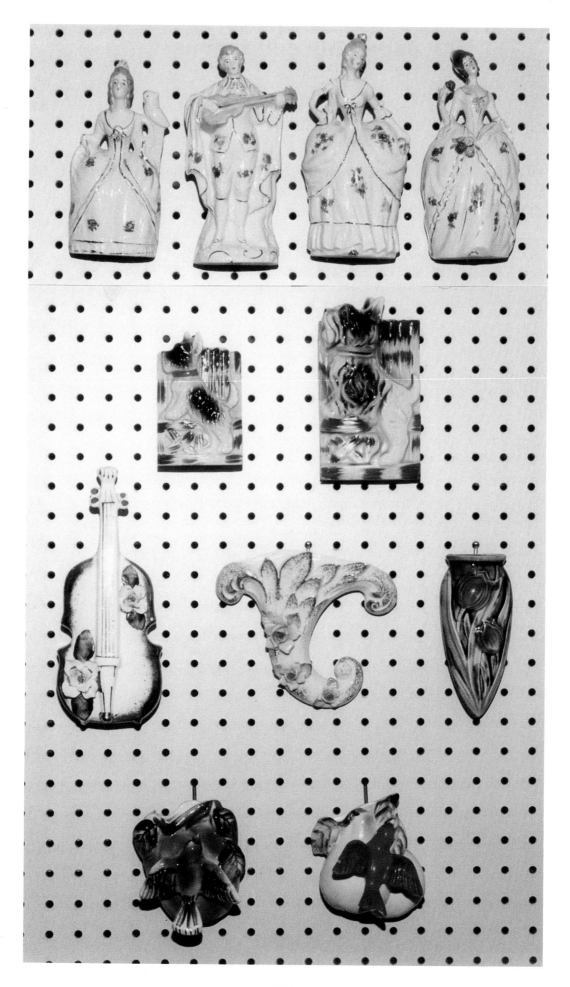

147

Japan Miscellaneous

ROW 1:

1. Young man with top hat, trimmed with gold, marked with a red foil label "UCAGCO CERAMICS JAPAN". **$20 - 25**

2. Black woman with red glass earrings, trimmed with gold, marked with a gold foil label "MADE IN JAPAN", it also has a black ink stamp "8A170". **$30 - 35**

3. Young lady with black hat, trimmed with gold, marked with a red foil label "UCAGCO CERAMICS JAPAN". **$20 - 25**

Priced per pair – **$45 - 55**

ROW 2:

1. Colorful girl head, marked with a black ink stamp "BETSON'S HAND-PAINTED JAPAN". **$20 - 25**

2. Small lady head, marked with a red ink stamp "QUALITY GUARANTEED JAPAN". **$15 - 20**

3. Colorful girl head, trimmed with gold, marked with a silver foil label "Hand-painted PICO JAPAN". **$20 - 25**

ROW 3:

1. Harlequin man, trimmed with gold, marked with a red ink stamp "MADE IN JAPAN". **$30 - 40**

2. Nude lady, aqua color, marked with a black ink stamp "MADE IN JAPAN". **$25 - 35**

3. Harlequin woman, trimmed with gold marked same as #1. **$30 - 40**

Price per pair – **$65 - 85**

ROW 4:

1 & 2. Pair of Native heads, marked with brown ink stamp "JAPAN". each – **$25 - 30**

Price per pair – **$50 - 60**

3. Small girl head, marked with a black ink stamp "JAPAN". **$20 - 25**

4. Woman with glasses, marked with a paper label "JAPAN". **$25 - 30**

149

Japan Miscellaneous

ROW 1:

1. Green fan with purple flowers, trimmed with gold, marked with a foil label "Lefton China Hand-painted Japan".   **$25 - 30**

2. Brown house trimmed with blue, marked with a blue paper label "JAPAN", and also marked with a black ink stamp "H332".   **$10 - 15**

3. Small brown cabin with chimney, marked with a black ink stamp "JAPAN".   **$10 - 15**

4. Lemon with leaves, marked with a blue paper label "JAPAN".   **$20 - 25**

ROW 2:

1. Young boy with a black hat, looking at the young girl, marked with a black ink stamp "JAPAN".   **$20 - 25**

2. Young girl watching the man in the toilet stool, marked with a black ink stamp "MADE IN JAPAN".   Price per pair – **$45 - 55**   **$20 - 25**

3. Man standing in toilet stool, marked with a blue paper label "MADE IN JAPAN". On the rim of the stool in black letters "GOODBYE CRUEL WORLD".   **$15 - 20**

ROW 3:

1. White two piece lavabo, floral design, trimmed with gold, marked with silver foil label "Wales MADE IN JAPAN".   **$25 - 35**

2. Parrot, multicolored, sitting on the blue limb, 7 1/2" tall, marked with black ink stamp "MADE IN JAPAN".   **$40 - 50**

3. Baby elephant, grey with gold trim, 4" tall, unmarked. The small size indicates possibly made in Japan.   **$35 - 40**

4. Triple style wall pocket, marked with a black ink stamp "MADE IN JAPAN".   **$30 - 40**

JAPAN NORITAKE

The Noritake Company was founded in 1904 by Baron Ichizaemon Morimura, and has devoted itself to making the finest china possible through the years and continues with the tradition today. The wall pockets we find today were made through the twenties and thirties and certainly show the superior quality of the Noritake Company.

ROW 1:

1. White luster with two blue birds, gold trim, and marked with a red ink stamp "NORITAKE M HANDPAINTED MADE IN JAPAN".   **$175 - 200**

2. Gold luster with two butterflies. The pocket has two handles on the side, marked with a red ink stamp "NORITAKE M HANDPAINTED MADE IN JAPAN".   **$200 - 225**

3. Gold luster with two grey birds, gold trim, marked with a red ink stamp "NORITAKE M HANDPAINTED MADE IN JAPAN".   **$175 - 200**

ROW 2:

1. Red luster with long tailed bird, gold trim, marked with a green ink stamp "NORITAKE M HANDPAINTED MADE IN JAPAN".   **$125 - 150**

2. Blue luster with figural lady, gold trim, and marked with a red ink stamp "NORITAKE M HANDPAINTED MADE IN JAPAN".   **$325 - 350**

3. Blue luster with multicolored parrot, gold trim, marked with a green ink stamp "NORITAKE M HANDPAINTED MADE IN JAPAN".   **$125 - 150**

ROW 3:

1. Blue luster with figural butterfly and bee, marked with a red ink stamp "NORITAKE M HANDPAINTED MADE IN JAPAN".   **$100 - 125**

2. Gold luster with multicolored scene, marked inside, green ink stamp "NORITAKE M HANDPAINTED MADE IN JAPAN".   **$225 - 250**

3. Gold and pearl luster, figural butterfly and bee with floral design, marked with red ink stamp "NORITAKE M HANDPAINTED MADE IN JAPAN".   **$100 - 125**

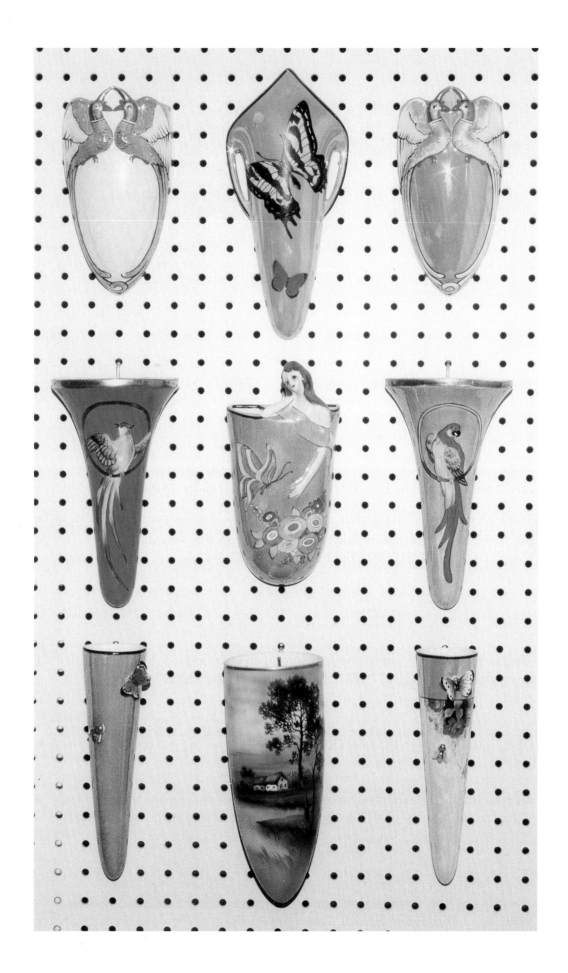

Japan Noritake

ROW 1:

1. Yellow and red luster with floral design, marked with a red ink stamp "NORITAKE M HANDPAINTED MADE IN JAPAN".   **$75 - 85**

2. Red and green luster with floral jack-in-the-pulpit design and other flowers, marked with a red ink stamp "NORITAKE M HANDPAINTED MADE IN JAPAN".   **$250 - 275**

3. Blue and Pearl luster, multicolored flowers, marked with a red ink stamp "NORITAKE M HANDPAINTED MADE IN JAPAN".   **$75 - 85**

ROW 2:

1. Blue luster with red trim, marked with a green ink stamp "NORITAKE M HANDPAINTED MADE IN JAPAN".   **$55 - 60**

2. Blue and white luster with large red flower, marked with a red ink stamp "NORITAKE M HANDPAINTED MADE IN JAPAN".   **$55 - 60**

3. Solid colored gold luster, marked with a green ink stamp "NORITAKE M HANDPAINTED MADE IN JAPAN".   **$55 - 60**

ROW 3:

1. Multicolored luster with house and country scene, marked with a red ink stamp "NORITAKE M HANDPAINTED MADE IN JAPAN".   **$75 - 80**

2. Red luster with blue, white and pink flowers, marked with a red ink stamp "NORITAKE M HANDPAINTED MADE IN JAPAN".   **$90 - 100**

3. Multicolored luster with a swan on a pond scene, marked with a green ink stamp "NORITAKE M HANDPAINTED MADE IN JAPAN".   **$80 - 90**

NOTE:
The Noritake Company used many variations in their backstamps, but until 1953 the M in a wreath was used on most of the wall pockets we find today, after 1953 the M was changed to an N.

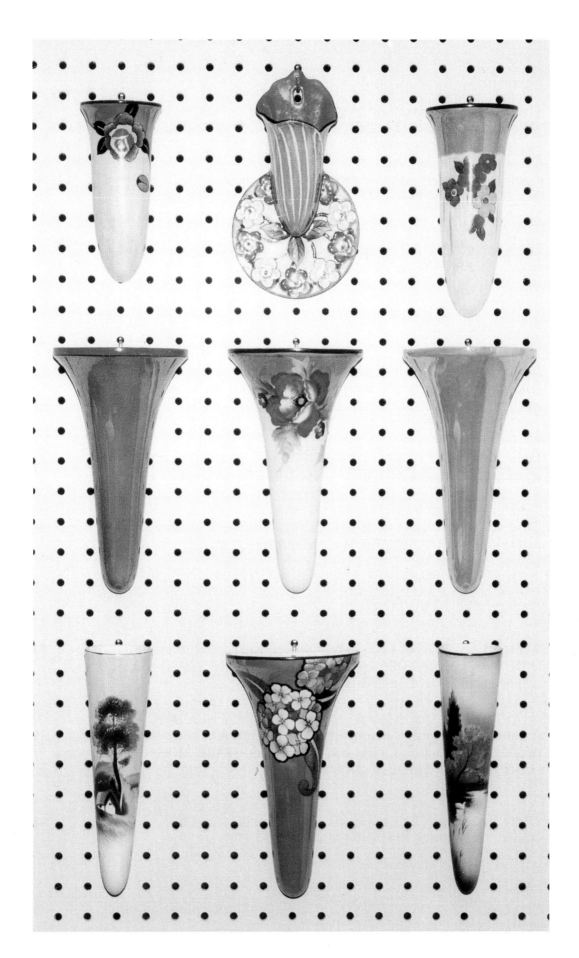

Japan Noritake

ROW 1:

    1. Gold luster with swan on pond scene, marked with a red ink stamp "NORITAKE M HANDPAINTED MADE IN JAPAN".   **$75 - 85**

    2. Grey pearl luster with two figural flowers, marked with a red ink stamp "NORITAKE M HANDPAINTED MADE IN JAPAN".   **$125 - 150**

    3. Gold and white luster with blue flower, marked with a red ink stamp "NORITAKE M HANDPAINTED MADE IN JAPAN".   **$75 - 85**

ROW 2:

    1. White luster with yellow and brown trim and bright multi-colored flowers, marked with a red ink stamp "NORITAKE M HANDPAINTED MADE IN JAPAN".   **$80 - 90**

    2. Light blue luster with long tailed bird and handles, marked with a red ink stamp "NORITAKE M HANDPAINTED MADE IN JAPAN".   **$200 - 225**

    3. Blue and pearl luster with red and white flowers, marked with a red ink stamp "NORITAKE M HANDPAINTED MADE IN JAPAN".   **$55 - 60**

ROW 3:

    1. White luster with art deco lady, marked with a red ink stamp "NORITAKE M HANDPAINTED MADE IN JAPAN" – (it also has five oriental figures) and then "No. 29812".   **$150 - 175**

    2. Aqua blue and yellow colors with a person in a canoe scene, marked inside with a green ink stamp "NORITAKE M HANDPAINTED MADE IN JAPAN".   **$225 - 250**

    3. White luster with fighting birds, marked with a red ink stamp "NORITAKE M HANDPAINTED MADE IN JAPAN".   **$100 - 125**

NOTE:

Noritake wall pockets with figural birds and butterflies and other figures applied to them bring a premium price.

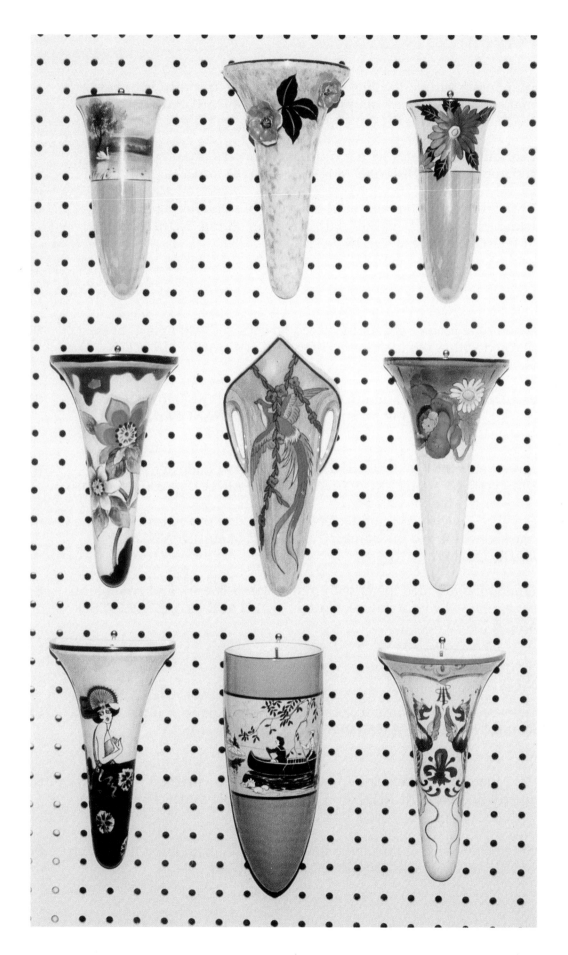

157

Japan Noritake

ROW 1:

1. Blue luster with old sailing ship at sea scene, trimmed with gold, marked with a red ink stamp "NORITAKE M HANDPAINTED MADE IN JAPAN".   **$125 - 150**

2. Pearl and blue luster with multicolored flowers, marked with a red ink stamp "NORITAKE M HANDPAINTED MADE IN JAPAN".   **$75 - 85**

3. Blue and gold luster with country scene of swan on pond, trimmed with gold, marked with a red ink stamp "NORITAKE M HANDPAINTED MADE IN JAPAN".   **$125 - 150**

ROW 2:

1. Small blue luster with multicolored flowers and two figural bees, marked with a red ink stamp "NORITAKE M HANDPAINTED MADE IN JAPAN".   **$125 - 150**

2. Small red luster with multicolored flowers and two figural bees, marked with a red ink stamp "NORITAKE M HANDPAINTED MADE IN JAPAN".   **$125 - 150**

3. Blue luster with gold trim and a bird and flowers design, marked with a red ink stamp "NORITAKE M HANDPAINTED MADE IN JAPAN".   **$125 - 150**

4. Small red luster with multicolored flowers and two figural bees, marked with a red ink stamp "NORITAKE M HANDPAINTED MADE IN JAPAN".   **$125 - 150**

5. Small blue marbled luster with multicolored flowers and two figural bees, marked with a red ink stamp "NORITAKE M HANDPAINTED MADE IN JAPAN".   **$125 - 150**

ROW 3:

1. Yellow colored with multicolored flowers, marked with a red ink stamp "NORITAKE M HANDPAINTED MADE IN JAPAN".   **$80 - 90**

2. Gold luster with gold trim, multicolored flowers, marked with a green ink stamp "NORITAKE M HANDPAINTED MADE IN JAPAN".   **$125 - 150**

3. Green color with multicolored flowers, marked with a red ink stamp "NORITAKE M HANDPAINTED MADE IN JAPAN".   **$80 - 90**

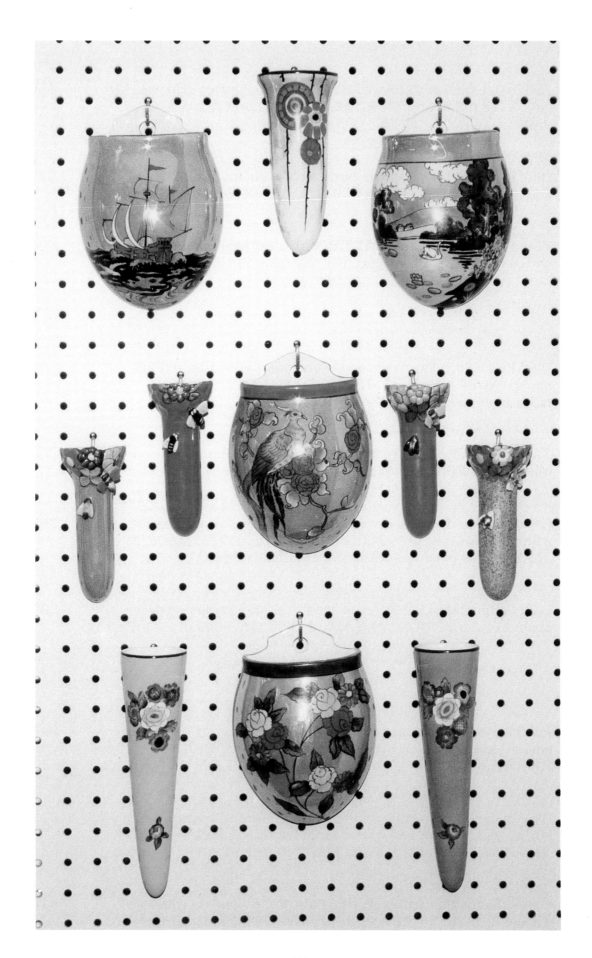

159

Japan Noritake

ROW 1:

1. Red luster with multicolored flowers, trimmed with gold, marked with a red ink stamp "NORITAKE M HANDPAINTED MADE IN JAPAN". **$80 - 90**

2. Blue luster with two orange birds, gold trim, and marked with a green ink stamp "NORITAKE M HANDPAINTED MADE IN JAPAN". **$175 - 200**

3. White luster, black and gold trim with a butterfly design, marked with a blue ink stamp "Legacy by Noritake © PHILIPPINES". **$60 - 70**

ROW 2:

1. Gold luster with swan on pond scene, marked with a red ink stamp "NORITAKE M HANDPAINTED MADE IN JAPAN". It has a store tag on back "CASTNER'S NASHVILLE, TENN.". **$85 - 95**

2. Blue luster with country scene, gold trim, marked with a red ink stamp "NORITAKE M HANDPAINTED MADE IN JAPAN". **$85 - 95**

3. Gold luster with multicolored flowers and gold trim, marked with a red ink stamp "NORITAKE M HANDPAINTED MADE IN JAPAN". This piece has white wavy vertical stripes. **$85 - 95**

4. Gold luster with a big red rose, gold trim and marked with a green ink stamp "NORITAKE M HANDPAINTED MADE IN JAPAN". **$80 - 90**

ROW 3:

1. Pearl luster with camel, pyramid and palm trees, trimmed with gold, 8" long, marked with a red ink stamp "NORITAKE M HANDPAINTED MADE IN JAPAN". **$150 - 175**

2. Blue luster, double type, and has a red rose and trimmed with lots of gold, 8" long x 6" wide. Marked with a red ink stamp "NORITAKE M HANDPAINTED MADE IN JAPAN". **$125 - 150**

3. Gold luster with country scene, gold trim, 8" long, marked with a red ink stamp "NORITAKE M HANDPAINTED MADE IN JAPAN". **$100 - 125**

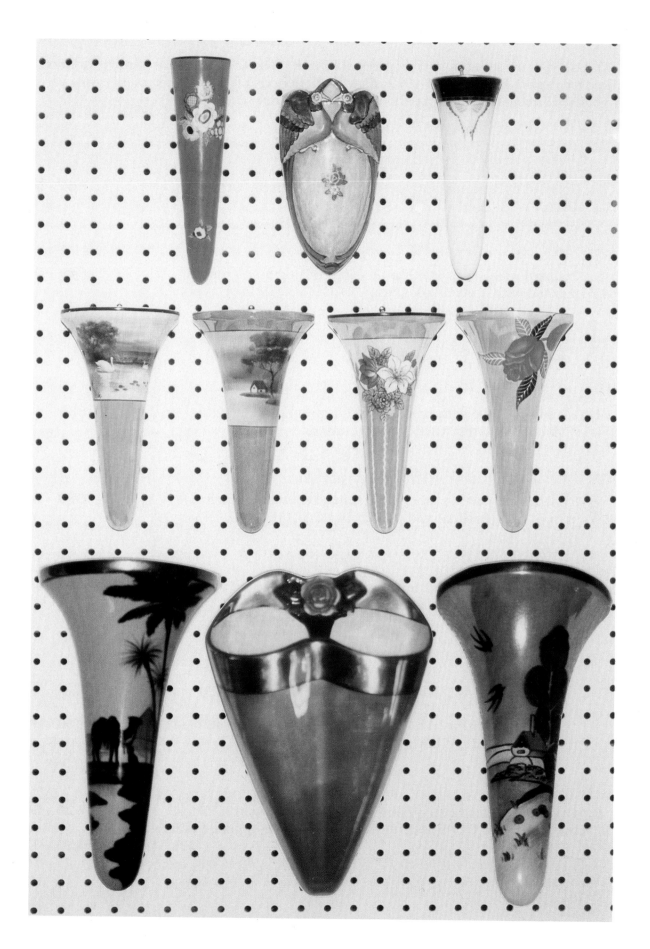

161

JAPAN OCCUPIED

Japan has made many different types of wall pockets, one of the hardest to find are the ones marked Occupied Japan, 1945-1952. As with all periods of Japan, they made some very beautiful wall pockets during this time, as shown in this chapter.

ROW 1:

    1. Colorful flying duck and crescent, mark incised "OCCUPIED JAPAN".   **$40 - 50**

    2. Colorful wise old owl with pine cones sitting on a crescent, marked with a black ink stamp "OCCUPIED JAPAN".   **$40 - 50**

ROW 2:

    1. White vase type with multicolored flowers, marked with a black ink stamp "OCCUPIED K JAPAN".   **$30 - 40**

    2. Dancing lady with a fancy frame, marked with a black ink stamp "510 Handpainted MADE IN OCCUPIED JAPAN".   **$60 - 75**

    3. White vase type with multicolored flowers, marked with a black ink stamp "OCCUPIED K JAPAN".   **$30 - 40**

ROW 3:

    1. Oriental boy sitting in a bamboo ring, marked with a black ink stamp "OCCUPIED JAPAN".   **$20 - 30**

    2. Oriental girl sitting in a bamboo ring, marked with a black ink stamp "OCCUPIED JAPAN". This is a true opposite pair.   **$20 - 30**

Price per pair – **$50 - 70**

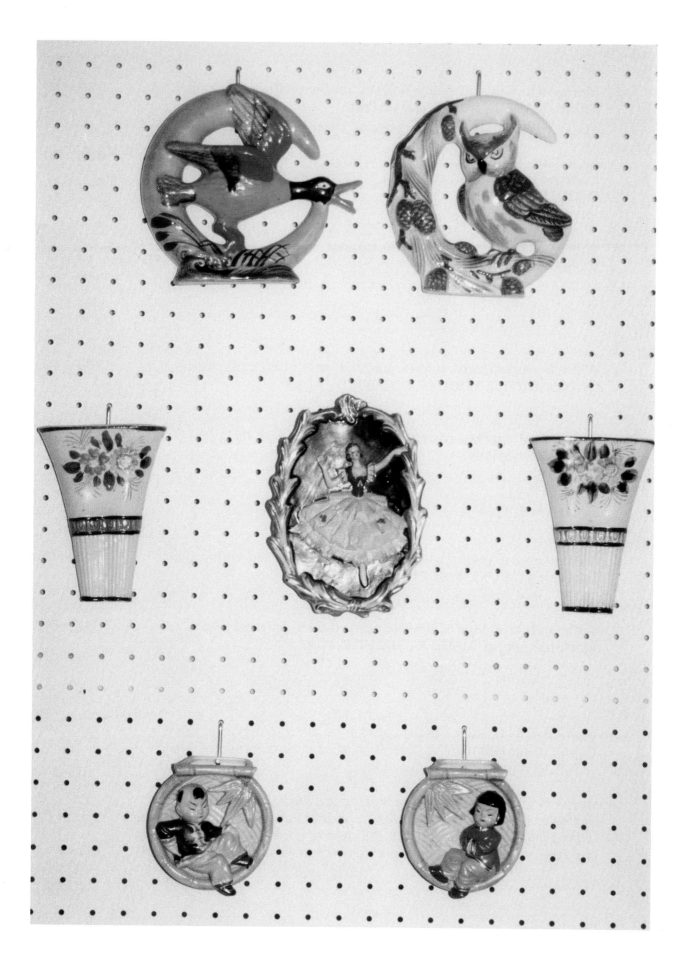

163

Japan Occupied

ROW 1:

1. Black with pink and yellow flowers, marked with a black ink stamp "MADE IN OCCUPIED JAPAN".   **$30 - 40**

2. India lady with a red hat and four arms, riding an elephant, trimmed in gold, marked with a green ink stamp "MADE IN OCCUPIED JAPAN".   **$50 - 60**

3. This is a side view of #2, so you can see how delicate and unique this wall pocket is.

ROW 2:

1. White flower with red stripes, marked with a black ink stamp "HANDPAINTED MADE IN OCCUPIED JAPAN".   **$30 - 40**

2. A pink rose, marked with a red ink stamp "MADE IN OCCUPIED JAPAN".   **$30 - 40**

ROW 3:

1. Two swans on a pond with water lily pads, marked with a black ink stamp "MADE IN OCCUPIED JAPAN".   **$35 - 45**

2. Tulip with little blue and white applied bird, marked with a black ink stamp "MADE IN OCCUPIED JAPAN".   **$40 - 50**

NOTE:

An often asked question – Is the color of the ink a wall pocket from Japan is marked with an indication of when a piece was made?

Answer – No. I have seen wall pockets made during the Nippon years, Noritake, Occupied, Made in Japan and Japan, in all colors. At one time I was lead to believe that the color of ink indicated the period a piece was made, and it may in other countries, but not Japan.

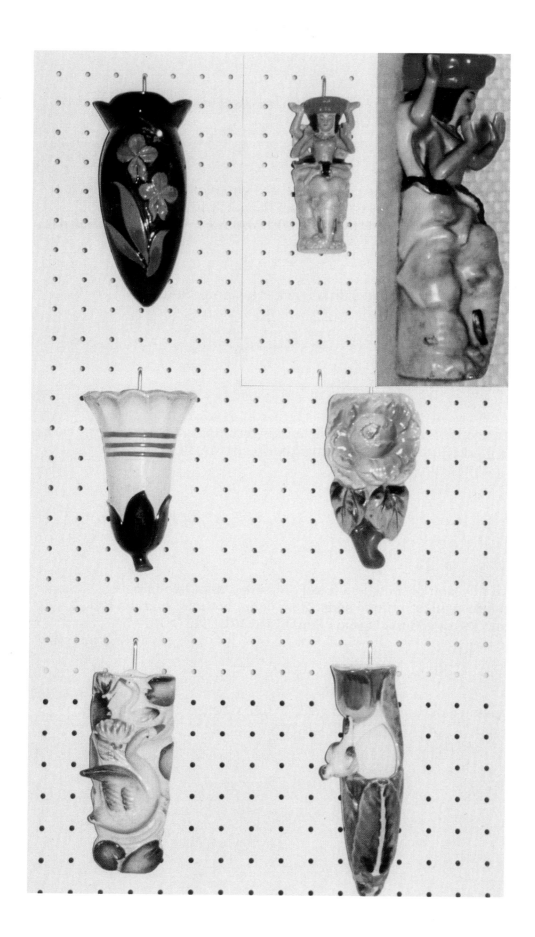

Japan Occupied

ROW 1:

1. Bird with a long beak, very colorful, marked with a black ink stamp "MADE IN OCCUPIED JAPAN". **$30 - 35**

2 & 3. A pair of tiny vase type pockets, yellow with white and blue stripes, (both are marked the same) marked with a red ink stamp "H. KATO MADE IN OCCUPIED JAPAN". each – **$25 - 35** Price per pair – **$50 - 70**

4. Colorful goose, marked with a black ink stamp "MADE IN OCCUPIED JAPAN". **$30 - 35**

ROW 2:

A true opposite pair, blue birds on tree stumps, 7" long, both are marked with red ink stamps that read "MADE IN OCCUPIED JAPAN". each – **$35 - 45** Priced per pair – **$80 - 100**

ROW 3:

1 & 2. Two tiny wall pockets in a hand are better than two hanging in some mall or antique shop, 2 1/2" long, both are marked the same with a red ink stamps "MADE IN OCCUPIED JAPAN". each – **$25 - 35** Priced per pair – **$50 - 70**

3. Dancing lady trimmed with gold, 7" tall, marked with a blue ink stamp "MADE IN OCCUPIED JAPAN". **$50 - 60**

167

McCOY POTTERY

W. Nelson McCoy and W.F. McCoy started the first Pottery in Putman, Ohio in 1848. The J.W. McCoy Pottery Company was founded in Roseville, Ohio in 1899, with George Brush becoming General Manager in 1909. In 1912 the name of the pottery became The Brush-McCoy Pottery Company and in 1925 it was changed again to The Brush Pottery, continuing until 1982 when it closed. In the meantime, the Nelson McCoy Sanitary Stoneware Company was founded in 1910, and in 1933 the company reorganized and became the Nelson McCoy Pottery Company. It was sold to the Lancaster Colony Corporation in the mid 1970's.

ROW 1:

1. Blue fan, marked with raised letters *"McCoy USA"*, made in 1956.   **$40 - 50**

2. Gold (Brocade) fan, marked with a gold stamp "GOLD 24 K", and   **$45 - 55**
    also marked with raised letters *"McCoy USA"*, made in 1957.

ROW 2:

1. Lady with hat and bow, white with red cold paint, mark impressed   **$40 - 50**
    "McCoy", made in 1943.

2. Cuckoo clock, brown/green with a yellow bird, and has green and   **$100 - 125**
    brown pendulums hanging on brass chains, marked with raised
    letters *"McCoy"*, made in 1952.

3. Clown with hat and collar, white with some red cold paint, mark   **$75 - 110**
    impressed *"McCoy"*, made in 1943.

ROW 3:

1. A brown/yellow basketweave design pocket, marked with raised   **$65 - 80**
    letters *"McCoy USA"*, and the original price tag is on the back
    that reads "DUCKWALL'S 98¢", made in 1956.

2. A yellow butterfly, with an incised mark *"NM"*, (Nelson McCoy),   **$200 - 300**
    early 1940's.

NOTE:

The butterfly wall pocket is one we were not even aware of until recently. Thanks to two McCoy collectors, we saw pictures of them finally. We found this one in a shop in Springfield, MO. The owner said it had been hanging there on a back wall for about six years. Priced at $10, Marvin had the nerve to ask for a 10% discount and got it.

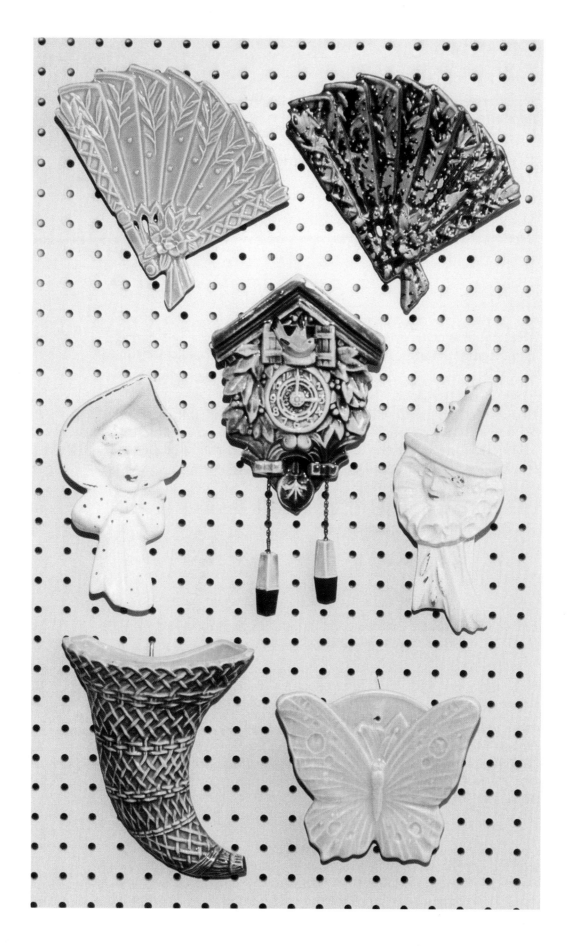

169

McCoy Pottery

ROW 1:

    1. Black trivet with white love birds, marked with raised letters   **$50 - 85**
       "McCoy U.S.A.", made in 1953.

    2. A yellow trivet with brown owls, marked with raised letters   **$50 - 85**
       "McCoy U.S.A", 1953.

    3. Black trivet with grey iron, marked with raised letters   **$40 - 75**
       "McCoy U.S.A.", made in 1953.

ROW 2:

    1. A yellow pear with green leaves and a brown stem, not marked.   **$50 - 60**
       The original selling price is ink stamped on the back 69¢, made
       in 1953.

    2. Brush-McCoy, green with embossed flowers, mark impressed   **$35 - 40**
       "MADE IN USA". This is called "KOLORKRAFT" and made in
       1929. This piece has the long mold marks on the back like
       the McCoy Mexican Man.

    3. Green trivet with black iron, marked with raised letters   **$40 - 75**
       "McCoy USA., made in 1953.

ROW 3:

    1. Brush-McCoy, large white cornucopia, mark impressed "MADE   **$25 - 30**
       IN USA", made in the mid 1950's.

    2. Half urn, pink with dark grey speckles, marked with raised   **$30 - 45**
       letters *"McCoy USA"*.

    3. Brush-McCoy, small white cornucopia, mark is impressed   **$20 - 25**
       "MADE IN USA". Both of the cornucopias have the long mold
       marks on the back like the Kolorkraft, the McCoy Mexican
       Man, and the Shawnee daffodil.

NOTE:

Putting a price on McCoy wall pockets is very hard. The prices vary so much from one area to another. What we have done is take the prices that have been given to us by collectors and dealers and average them out, and hope that you will only look at these prices as a guide, not as the final price.

171

McCoy Pottery

ROW 1:

1. Yellow leaves, shaded colors, marked with raised letters *"McCoy"*, made in the 1950's. — **$35 - 50**

2. Yellow leaves and berries, no markings. This one is hard to find, made in 1935. — **$150 - 200**

3. Mauve and ivory leaves, marked with raised letters *"McCoy"*, made in the 1950's. — **$35 - 50**

ROW 2:

1. Blossomtime, white with pink blossoms, marked with raised letters *"McCoy"*, made in 1947. — **$75 - 90**

2. Yellow lily with green leaves, marked with raised letters *"McCoy"*. Some collectors call this piece "The McCoy Easter Lily", made in 1948. — **$65 - 75**

3. Blossomtime, yellow with pink blossoms, marked with raised letters *"McCoy"*, made in 1947. — **$75 - 90**

ROW 3:

1. Cornucopia, black with white and grey flower decals accented with gold trim, no markings. — **$30 - 50**

2. Cornucopia, white with white and blue flower decals, no markings. This piece and the one above were made in the early 1980's. Some McCoy collectors refer to these as the "Tongue". — **$30 - 50**

NOTE:

During the late 1920's and into the 1930's, times were hard for the potteries in the United States, not marking their pieces was one of the ways they used to save money. Several potteries even formed a company and used a common catalog. Some of the potteries also sold wares from other potteries in their showrooms. So it is understandable why we have a hard time trying to identify some of the unmarked pieces we find today.

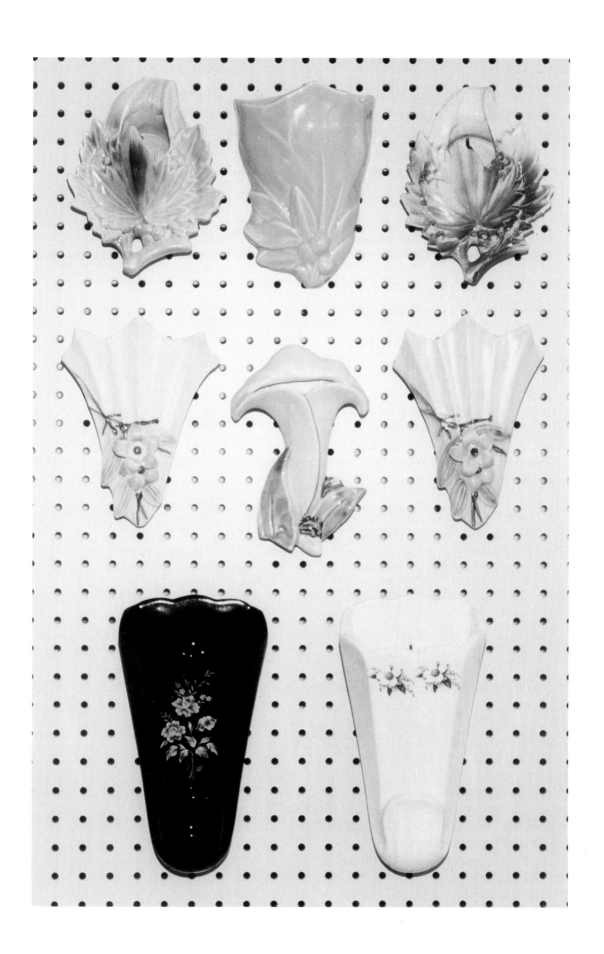

McCoy Pottery

ROW 1:

    1. Pink with flower and leaves design, mark impressed "MADE IN   **$30 - 40**
USA". This piece has the long mold marks on the back like
the "Brush KOLORKRAFT", McCoy Mexican man and cornucopia. We don't know for sure who made this, but it is collected
as a McCoy by some McCoy collectors.

    2. Umbrella, gold brocade, marked with gold stamp "GOLD 24 K",   **$50 - 75**
and also marked with raised letters *"McCoy USA"*, 1957.

    3. Brush-McCoy, large yellow cornucopia, the mark is impressed   **$25 - 30**
"MADE IN USA". This piece has the long mold marks like #1 above.

ROW 2:

    1. Small lily with leaves, light green, marked with incised *"NM"*,   **$50 - 100**
made in the early 1940's.

    2. Green mail box, marked with raised letters *"McCoy USA"*,   **$75 - 90**
made in 1951.

    3. White lily with leaves, marked with incised *"NM"*, made in the   **$50 - 100**
early 1940's.

ROW 3:

    1. Blue Dutch shoe, marked with raised letters *"McCoy"*, made in 1947.   **$30 - 45**

    2. Cornucopia, white with blue speckles, no markings, early 1980's.   **$30 - 50**

    3. Bellows with flowers and leaves design, marked with raised letters   **$75 - 90**
"McCoy USA", made in 1956.

NOTE:
The following is a list of McCoy wall pockets shown in our first book.

1. Bird on bird bath	8. Lady with hat
2. Bird on flower	9. Lily
3. Blossom flower	10. Pear
4. Clown with hat and collar	11. Trivet/owls
5. Dutch shoe	12. Umbrella (black)
6. Fan (blue)	13. Umbrella (gold brocade)
7. Grapes	

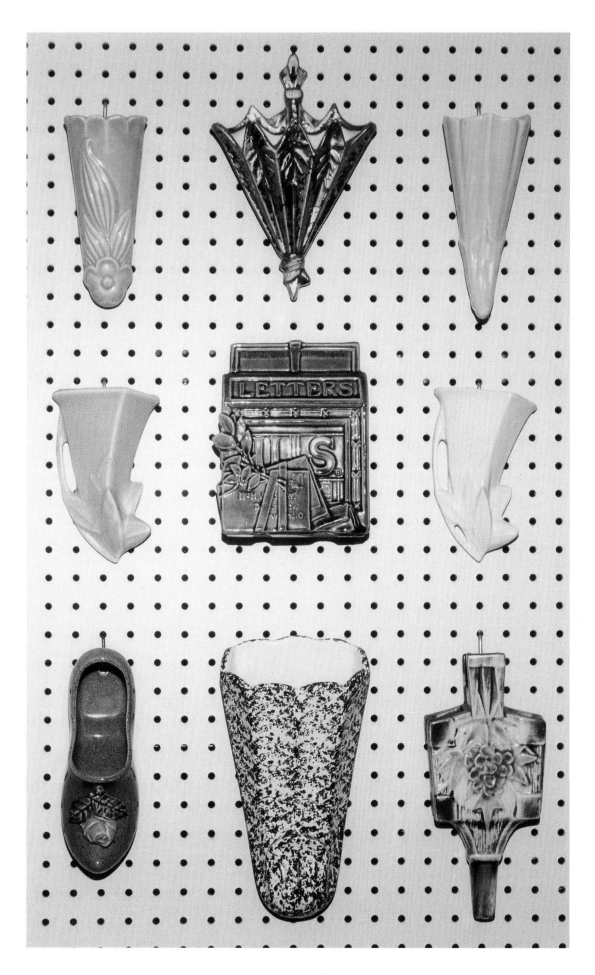

175

McCoy Pottery

ROW 1:

    1. Purple grapes with leaves, no markings, made in 1953.   **$65 - 85**

    2. Bananas with leaves, no markings, 1953.   **$85 - 100**

    3. Green grapes with leaves, no markings, made in 1953.   **$75 - 100**

ROW 2:

    Three red apples with leaves, some color variation, no markings, 1953.   **$50 - 65**

ROW 3:

    1. Bird on a flower, marked with raised letters *"McCoy"*, made in 1948.   **$40 - 55**

    2. Bird on a bird bath, marked with raised letters *"McCoy"*, made in 1949.   **$50 - 100**

    3. Blossom, no markings, made in 1946.   **$15 - 20**

NOTE:

The following is a list of Brush/McCoy wall pockets known to us that are not in our first book or this book II.

1. ACORN, 8" tall.
2. CIRCLES, small, 6" tall, 1939.
3. CIRCLES, large #588-8" tall.
4. CORNUCOPIA, (twister), 9 1/2" tall.
5. DRAGON FLY, plain, 10" tall.
6. DRAGON FLY, fancy decorated, 10" tall.
7. EARLY AMERICAN, white with blue floral, 9" tall, 1967.
8. THREE LEAVES/THREE BERRIES, 8" tall, late 1940's.
9. LION HEADS, two sizes, 6" and 7 1/2", 1929.
10. MATCH BOX HOLDER, old type with 13 vertical lines on front and the word "MATCHES", late 1920's to early 30's.
11. MATCH BOX HOLDER, new type with three vertical panels that are rounded at the top of each panel.
12. MERMAID JEWELRY HOLDER, 5 1/2" tall.
13. LONG TAILED BIRD, 6" tall, 1929.
14. STARDUST HANGER, top piece 7 3/4" tall, mark incised "73-USA", the "S" is larger and backwards. The bottom piece is a 4 1/2" pot hanging from brass chains.
15. VASE TYPE, with scene of 4 white geese, grass and trees, 12" tall, marked with a paper label *"Mitusa* TRADE MARK". Made prior to 1920.

(There were numerous wall hanging salt boxes made in various patterns and in many colors).

177

McCoy Pottery

ROW 1:

1. Fancy vase type with leaves and blossoms, blue, 7 1/2" tall. Mark incised "*McCoy*".   **$175 - 250**

2. Orange with leaves, 7 1/2" tall, the orange color is cold paint, no markings, 1953.   **$65 - 85**

3. Plain vase type with leaves, blue color, 7 1/2" tall. Mark incised "*NM*".   **$150 - 200**

ROW 2:

1. Small lily with leaves, light blue color, 6" tall, mark incised "*NM*", early 1940's.   **$50 - 100**

2. Owl, Brush-McCoy, came in matte or glossy finish, 8" tall, 1927-1930.   **$125 - 150**

3. Mexican man holding hat, light blue, 7" tall, made in 1941.   **$50 - 75**

ROW 3:

1. Butterfly, light blue, 5 3/4" tall, mark incised "*NM*" (Nelson McCoy). Made in early 1940's.   **$200 - 300**

2. Violin, blue, 10 1/4" tall, made in 1957, also made in white, add $50-$75.   **$100 - 125**

ROW 4:

1. Brown boxer dog, "Brush", 7" tall, mark incised "542 USA", and also comes in grey color.   **$90 - 125**

2. Baby doll, "Brush" 6" tall, made 1978.   **$75 - 125**

3. Fish, white/green, "Brush", 7" tall.   **$75 - 110**

4. Puppy in dog house, "Brush" 7 1/2" tall.   **$90 - 125**

ROW 5:

1. Black and white spotted horse, "Brush", 6 1/2" tall.   **$100 - 125**

2. Flying duck, "Brush", 8" tall, comes in a matte and glossy finish.   **$75 - 85**

3. Small white bucking horse, "Brush", 6 1/2" tall.   **$85 - 100**

4. Large brown bucking horse, "Brush", 7 1/2" tall.   **$125 - 150**

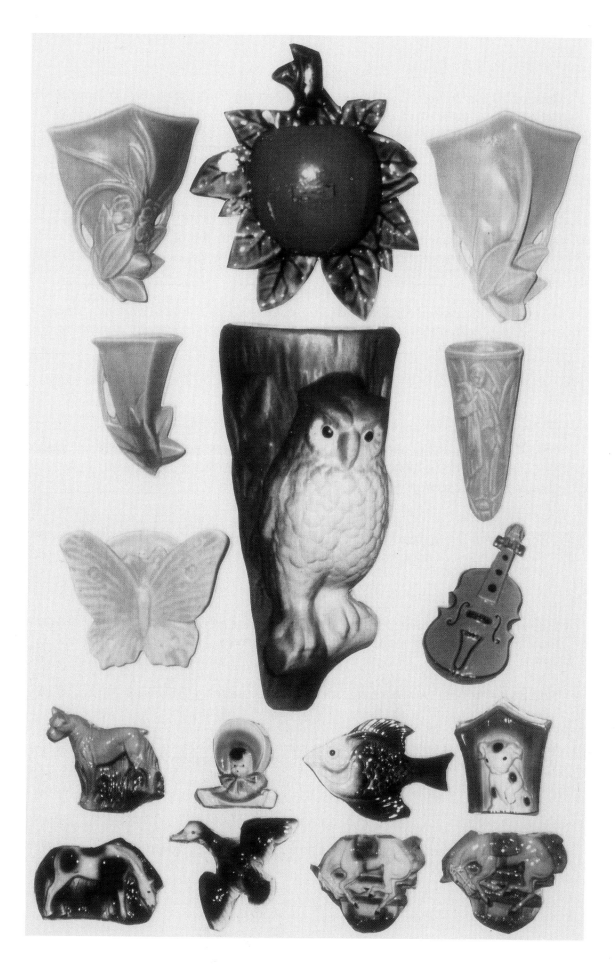

MEXICO, PHILIPPINES & PORTUGAL

Mexico

Mexico, of all the modern nations in the American Continent, has behind it the richest continuous artistic heritage. Many different art forms have flourished in the country. One of the most recognized being their pottery. A large percentage of the art ware produced in Mexico is made for the tourist trade. Pottery has been made in Mexico for hundreds of years.

Philippines

The Philippines are known for their hand crafting on wood, horns and even metal. Their bamboo huts are symbolic of their culture and is included in much of their artware.

Portugal

Pottery is an old custom for the Portuguese. In spite of the years spent under a dictatorship, they managed to produce many beautiful pieces, including some great wall pockets. Portugal is well known for their majolica.

ROW 1:

1. White diaper, marked with two paper labels "MADE IN PORTUGAL"   **$20 - 25**
   and "HEMISPHERE CORPORATION Kansas City, MO U.S.A.", and
   also is handpainted in red "MU-752".

2. Bunch of red beets, marked with a paper label "MADE IN PORTUGAL".   **$25 - 40**

ROW 2:

1. Pair of real bovine horns, hand carved and made in the "PHILIPPINES".   **$40 - 50**
   On each is a scene of a native hut and palm trees.

2. Red birds on nest, no marking. Identified as made in "MEXICO".   **$15 - 20**

3. Yellow birds on a nest, no markings. Identified as made in "MEXICO".   **$15 - 20**
   We have seen others like these plainly marked "MADE IN MEXICO".

ROW 3:

Double type pocket with Mexican scene, no markings. Identified   **$20 - 25**
as "MADE IN MEXICO".

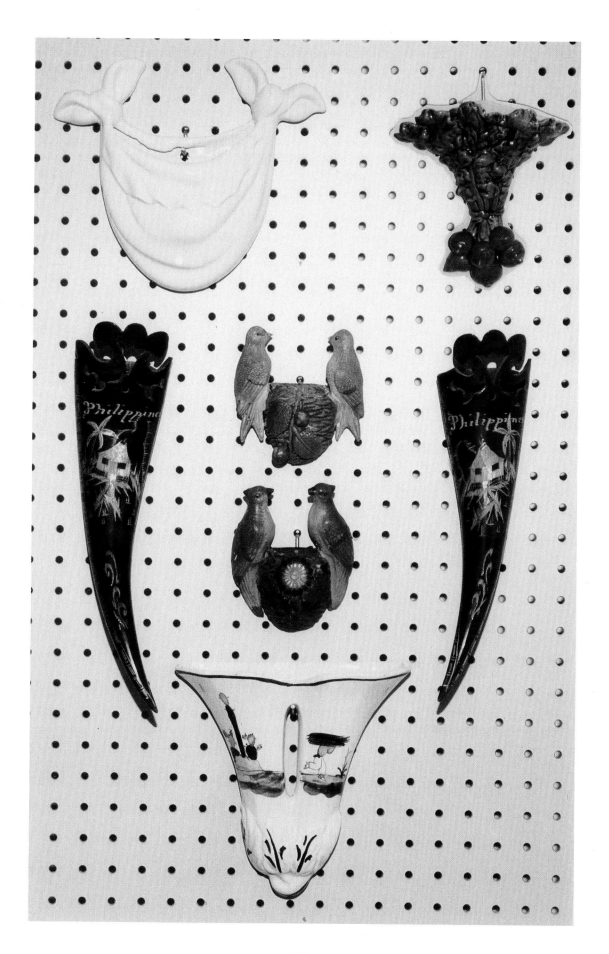

MISCELLANEOUS

The wall pockets in this chapter are ones we could not identify or did not have enough to put in a chapter of their own. It is very hard to identify some wall pockets because of the similarity in colors and glazes of the different potteries.

ROW 1:

    Dark green sea horse, no markings.   **$20 - 25**

ROW 2:

1. Green and chartreuse fish, no markings.   **$25 - 30**

2. Bird house, green with brown trim, no markings.   **$15 - 20**

ROW 3:

1. Angel Fish, white trimmed with green and gold, no markings.   **$10 - 15**

2. Lobster, multicolored browns, no markings.   **$20 - 25**

3. Colorful little fish, pink and yellow with gold trim, it also has three bubbles, no markings.   **$10 - 15**

ROW 4:

1. Basket, black with grey speckles, no markings.   **$20 - 25**

2. Rooster, yellow and green, no markings. It has the original price on back 49¢.   **$10 - 15**

3. Yellow bull head fish, trimmed with black and gold, no markings.   **$15 - 20**

183

Miscellaneous

ROW 1:

    1. Mauve colored pepper with green leaves. It has a delicate applied stem, marked with a black ink stamp "Klay Kraft, Milford, Nebraska".   **$25 - 30**

    2. Wren bird on a green leaf with red grapes, no markings, very good quality.   **$30 - 40**

    3. Red strawberry with green leaves, no markings.   **$25 - 30**

ROW 2:

    1. Light green apple and leaves, no markings.   **$20 - 25**

    2. Tree shape, green and white with brown pine cones, mark incised "Loveland Art Pottery - 122".   **$25 - 30**

    3. Dark green apple and leaves, mark impressed "© U.S.A.".   **$20 - 25**

ROW 3:

    1. Multicolored browns, mark incised "ROMCO U.S.A.", and it has a green glaze inside and also inside is a paper label reading "PINE SCENTED POTTERY WIPE WITH A DAMP CLOTH TO CLEAN. The fragrance is in the bottom on the outside of the pottery". The original selling price is on the back $1.98.   **$25 - 30**

    2. Large multicolored browns, decorated with pine cones and needles, marked with paper label inside "Hand-painted Original By The Artists of Rocky Mountain Pottery Co., Estes Park and Loveland, Colorado".   **$30 - 40**

    3. Multicolored browns, marked with a black ink stamp "MADE IN COLORADO". It has a green glaze inside, and also inside is a paper label "PINE SCENTED POTTERY WIPE WITH A DAMP CLOTH TO CLEAN. The fragrance is in the bottom on the outside of the pottery".   **$25 - 30**

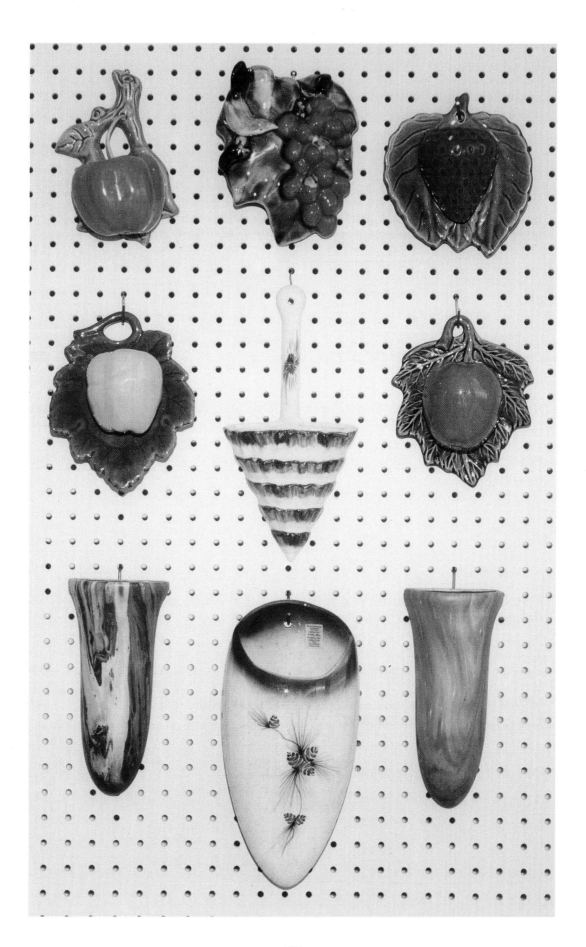

Miscellaneous

ROW 1:

    1. Swan, ivory color with gold trim, no markings.   **$25 - 30**

    2. Green pot with embossed design of a four leaf clover, no markings.   **$15 - 20**

    3. Swan, pink and black, no markings. This wall pocket and #1 were not marked, but we saw one in an Antique Mall with a paper label marked "Stanford Pottery, Sebring, Ohio", 1945-1961.   **$20 - 25**

ROW 2:

    1. Pink swan, trimmed with gold, no markings.   **$50 - 60**

    2. Swan, same as #1, but turned for a side view, no markings.   **$50 - 60**

    3. Black Pottery Wall Pocket, mark impressed "#436", very good quality.   **$40 - 50**

ROW 3:

    1. Dutch windmill clock, very colorful with a boy and a girl. The time is 8:22, no markings.   **$25 - 30**

    2. Upside down bell, trimmed with blue and gold. Hand-painted on the front with gold "BILL AND JUNE KRAMER, FEB. 8TH. 1935, NEVADA, MO.", and also marked on the back, hand-painted in black "HAPPY ANNIVERSARY".   **$10 - 15**

    3. Old oil lamp, yellow and black, no markings.   **$15 - 20**

Miscellaneous

ROW 1:

    1. Girls head, she's looking at the young boy, no markings.   **$15 - 20**

    2. Pink set includes –
        Wall Pocket, mark impressed "223".   **$15 - 20**
        Vase, mark impressed "905".   **$10 - 15**
        Candle Holders with red candles   **$10 - 15**
        Price per set – **$40 - 55**

    3. Boys head, looking at young girl, no markings.   **$15 - 20**

ROW 2:

    1. Art deco style wall pocket, grey color, no markings, good quality.   **$45 - 50**

    2. Leaves, multicolored yellow and brown, no markings. This piece is extra heavy and of good quality, it also has an original selling price on back $1.39, in pencil "1959".   **$25 - 30**

    3. Grey with flower design, mark incised "ATLANTIC © MOLD".   **$10 - 15**

ROW 3:

    1. Clock with birds, light blue, the time is 5:03, no markings.   **$25 - 30**

    2. Green and white pitcher with rose design, trimmed with gold, no markings.   **$20 - 25**

    3. Western saddle, aqua blue color, no markings.   **$30 - 35**

189

Miscellaneous

ROW 1:

    1. Electric lamp wall pocket without the shade. It is grey and mauve colored, mark incised "Bucking-ham".   **$25 - 30**

    2. Electric lamp wall pocket without the shade. It is yellow and green in color, with no markings.   **$25 - 30**

ROW 2:

    Brown owl sitting on a limb, no markings. This piece hangs in a metal holder.   **$25 - 30**

ROW 3:

    1. Light blue pot hanging in a brass colored metal holder with a leaf design, no markings.   **$15 - 20**

    2. Two-tone brown pot sitting in a brass colored metal holder with a scroll design, no markings.   **$15 - 20**

ROW 4:

    Electric clock with a green and white plastic cover. The green side pockets will hold water or dirt. The clock is marked with black letters "Telechron MADE IN USA". On the back side of the plastic cover it is marked in raised letters –   **$40 - 50**

        "REG. U.S. Telechron PAT. OFF.
        ELECTRIC CLOCK
        MODEL 2H39
        VOLTS 115 CYC. CO W2
        DEPARTMENT OF GENERAL ELECTRIC COMPANY
        ASHLAND, MASS. MADE IN U.S.A."

Notice the old style bakelite electric plug on the clock.

Miscellaneous

ROW 1:

    1. Blue and grey leaves, mark incised "Dryden".   **$25 - 30**

    2. Green 4-H wall pocket with a young girl and boy members, no markings. This has been identified as a "Dryden" made in Ellsworth, KS as a special order for the 4-H club. Dryden Pottery was founded by James Dryden in Ellsworth, Kansas in 1946 and moved to Hot Springs, Arkansas in 1956. The clay used in Kansas was a dark tan, and in Arkansas it is a white clay. This is one way to tell in which era a piece was made. Dryden specializes in "one of a kind" pieces.   **$40 - 50**

ROW 2:

    1. Pfaltzgraff wall pocket, white with a rose design, marked "© PFALTZGRAFF York, Pennsylvania USA", 1811-present.   **$25 - 30**

    2. Wild running Black Beauty horse, trimmed with gold, no markings.   **$30 - 35**

ROW 3:

    1. Head, terra cotta painted white, marked with a paper label "CIMARRON POTTERY $5.49 EACH".   **$10 - 15**

    2. Small green pocket highlighted with gold, brown glaze inside, no markings.   **$10 - 15**

    3. Head – same as #1.   **$10 - 15**

ROW 4:

    1. Owl in a tree, tan color, no markings.   **$20 - 25**

    2. Bamboo style design, tan and brown, no markings.   **$15 - 20**

    3. Brown tree limbs, no markings.   **$15 - 20**

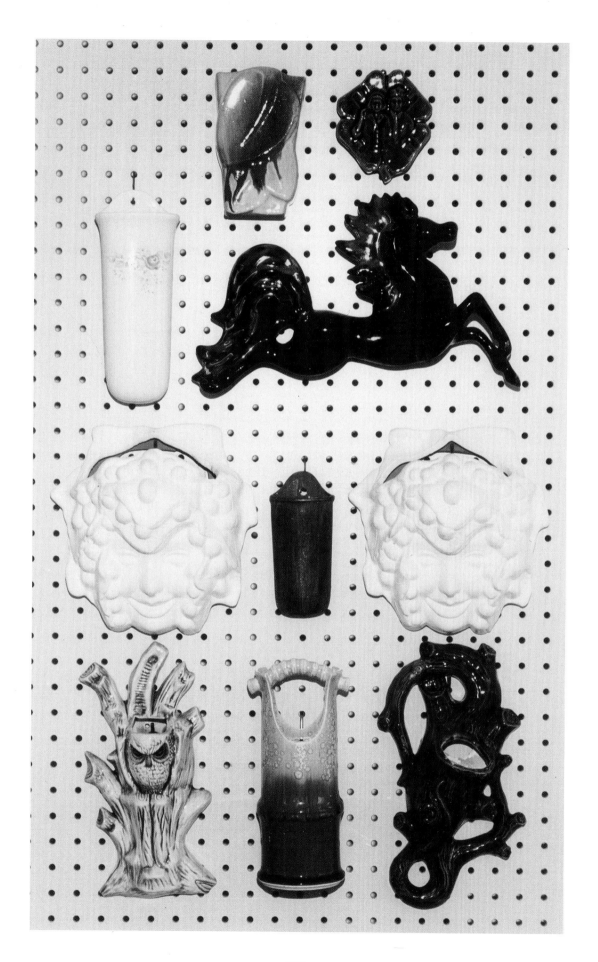

193

Miscellaneous

ROW 1:

1. Cup and saucer, white with yellow flowers, mark incised "CRAMER MOLD PS175".   **$5 - 10**

2. Cup, white trimmed with brown and cherries design, no markings.   **$10 - 15**

ROW 2:

1. Cup and saucer, green with yellow trim and flowers, no markings.   **$10 - 15**

2. Cup and saucer, ivory color trimmed with gold in a delicate flower pattern, mark incised "N.S. CO. Clev. O. U.S.A. S.P.3".   **$25 - 30**

ROW 3:

1. Cup and saucer, white trimmed with red, no markings. Identified as "CAMARK 150D". This piece was shown in the Camark chapter, shown again here for comparison with next cup in this row. Notice the difference in placement of the hole for hanging, and also where the handles on the cup are at the edge of the saucer.   **$25 - 30**

2. Cup and saucer, ivory color trimmed with a green and multicolored fruit and flowers, mark incised "N.S. Co. Clev. O. U.S.A. S.P.3".   **$25 - 30**

ROW 4:

Cup and saucer, green and brown glaze, mark impressed "A.R. COLE POTTERY SANFORD, N.C.". The A.R. Cole Pottery was started in 1934 by Mr. Arthur Cole. Mr. Cole came from a long line of potters, his pottery was hand thrown. After his death in 1974, his daughters took over the pottery and continue to run it. His son also follows in his father's footsteps and has a pottery of his own.   **$20 - 25**

195

Miscellaneous

ROW 1:

1. Plastic silhouette creamer, black with ivory colored pot for flowers, no markings.   **$3 - 5**

2. Plastic silhouette style, decorated with red birds and black leaves, and has a white pot for flowers, no markings.   **$15 - 20**

3. Plastic silhouette sugar bowl, black with ivory colored pot for flowers, no markings. This is part of a set with #1.   **$3 - 5**

   Price per set – **$7 - 10**

ROW 2:

1. Multicolored doll, made of papier-mache, no markings.   **$15 - 20**

2. Plastic silhouette with boy sitting on a fence picking fruit from a tree. It has a white pot for flowers, no markings.   **$15 - 20**

3. Plastic silhouette of coffee pot, black with white pot for flowers, no markings.   **$4 - 7**

ROW 3:

1. Yellow plastic teapot with plastic salt and pepper shakers, marked with raised letters "S. P. 6 SUPERLON, CHICAGO, ILL. MADE IN U.S.A. PAT. PEND.".   **$10 - 15**

2. Plastic pot, southwestern design, white with coral and aqua colors, marked inside the pot "© 3251 BURWOOD PRODUCTS CO. MADE IN U.S.A. MCMXCI".   **$5 - 7**

3. Red plastic teapot with a glass salt and pepper shaker, marked with raised letters "S.P. 4 SUPERLON, CHICAGO ILL. MADE IN U.S.A. PAT. PEND.". This pair of salt and pepper shakers have red plastic shaker tops and red painted dots on the glass part.   **$15 - 20**

197

Miscellaneous

ROW 1:

    1. Copper plate with scene of a hunter with a gun and two dogs. It   **$10 - 20**
        has a copper pot for flowers, no markings found.

    2. Solid copper in the shape of a lily with leaves. The mark is   **$30 - 35**
        engraved "Gregorian Copper 803 ®".

ROW 2:

    Pair of metal wall hangers with brass pots for growing   each – **$10 - 15**
    flowers. They have black wire frames decorated with metal
    leaves and each have three brass knobs. They are both marked
    on the bottom of the metal pots with raised letters "ARTISTIC
    WIRE PROD. EAST HAMPTON, CONN".   Price per pair – **$20 - 30**

ROW 3:

    1 & 3. A pair of hammered brass pictures of an Oriental girl and   each – **$20 - 25**
        boy with solid brass pots for growing flowers. They have black
        metal frames that are like old picture frames with black
        cardboard on the back to hold the copper pictures inside, no
        markings.   Price per pair – **$50 - 60**

    2. Solid brass cone shape with fan design on top rim, extra heavy,   **$15 - 20**
        no markings.

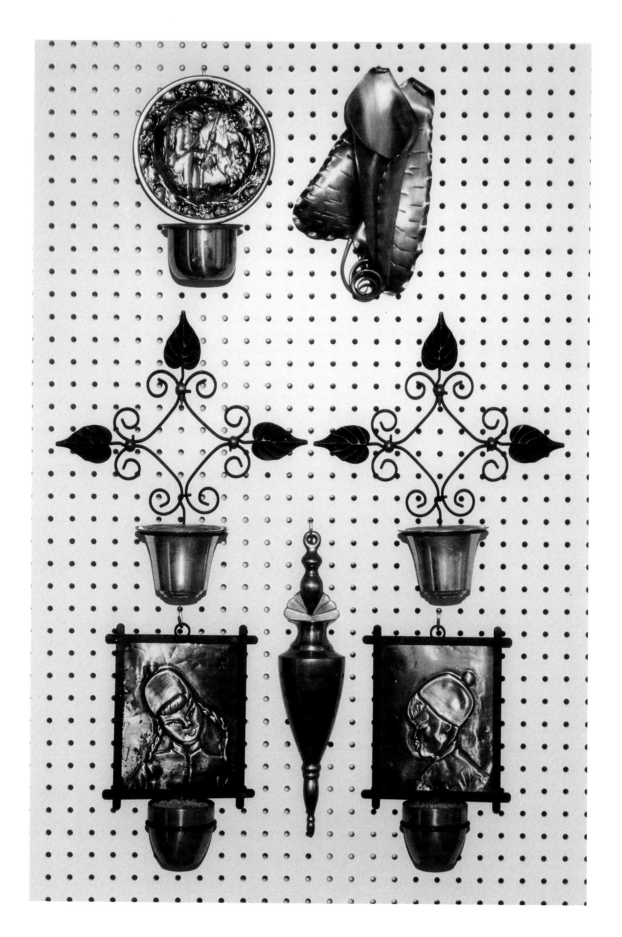

199

Miscellaneous

ROW 1:

    1. Old wood handmade wall pocket, with a dutch girl, most likely   **$20 - 25**
made to hold combs or papers, no markings.

    2. Wood scissors holder with a pink rose design, no markings.   **$15 - 20**

    3. Old wood handmade wall pocket, white colored with red, yellow   **$15 - 20**
and green apples, made to hold combs or papers, no markings.

ROW 2:

    1. Old wood handmade flower pot holder, shaped like a tulip,   **$5 - 10**
no markings.

    2. Patio wall pocket with lizard design. This piece is extra heavy   **$10 - 15**
and has a drain hole in the bottom, no markings.

    3. Old wood handmade flower pot holder, same as #1.   **$5 - 10**
Price per pair – **$10 - 20**

ROW 3:

    1. Chalk, red apple match holder or incense burner, no markings.   **$15 - 20**

    2 & 3. Chalk, a pair of colorful Oriental people, no markings.   each – **$15 - 20**
Price per pair – **$35 - 45**

ROW 4:

    1. Chalk wall pocket, made to look like "WELLER ROBA" pattern,   **$15 - 20**
no markings.

    2. Large chalk wall pocket with three cherubs, that has a drain hole   **$20 - 25**
in the bottom, no markings. This piece was bought at an estate
auction and was hanging on the front porch, it looked like it had
hung there for a very long time.

    3. Chalk, same as #1.   **$15 - 20**

Miscellaneous

ROW 1:

1. Orange fruit with leaves, no markings. $15 - 20

2. Yellow, decorated with a lady in a blue dress and a rooster, marked with a red ink stamp "Chinese letters and MADE IN CHINA". This piece is a new China import. $25 - 40

3. Gold brocade decorated apple, the mark is stamped in gold "24KT. gold MADE IN U.S.A.". $25 - 30

ROW 2:

1. Peacock, blue and yellow, no markings. $20 - 25

2. Green strawberry pot, mark incised "Riddell", made in California. We could not find any more information on this pottery. $20 - 25

3. Square pocket with "FATHER" on the front, gold trim, no markings. $15 - 20

ROW 3:

1. Brown house, no markings. $10 - 15

2. Yellow with green design, no markings. $10 - 15

3. Aqua colored leaves, no markings. $10 - 15

ROW 4:

1. Double morning glory, dark pink, marked with a blue ink stamp "ABINGDON U.S.A.". This wall pocket does not have a number impressed into it like the other two Abingdons on this page. $50 - 60

2. White and yellow lily, marked with a blue ink stamp "ABINGDON U.S.A.", and also impressed "586". $60 - 75

3. Pink morning glory, marked with a blue ink stamp "ABINGDON U.S.A.", and also impressed "377". $40 - 50

Abingdon Pottery of Abingdon, Illinois started making art pottery in 1934. The factory ceased production of the art pottery in 1950.

Miscellaneous

ROW 1:

    1. Yellow and mauve colored flower with mauve leaves, no markings.   **$20 - 25**

    2. Two kids with a spotted dog, no markings.   **$25 - 30**

    3. Basket with multicolored flowers, no markings.   **$15 - 20**

ROW 2 & 3.

    Set consisting of a white shelf, marked "© BURWOOD PRODUCTS CO. 2924 B MCMLXXXVIII MADE IN U.S.A.".   **$5 - 7**

    Left mitten with red decoration, marked with "© BURWOOD PRODUCTS CO. 3232-2 MCMXCL MADE IN U.S.A.".   **$5 - 7**

    Right mitten with red decoration, marked with red decoration, marked "© BURWOOD PRODUCTS CO. 3232 MCMXCL MADE IN U.S.A.".   **$5 - 7**

Price per set – **$15 - 25**

    Light tan font type pocket with black trim, no markings.   **$15 - 20**

ROW 4:

    1. White and blue leaves, no markings.   **$5 - 10**

    2. Aqua blue with large panel of gold brocade, marked with a gold ink stamp "24 KT. GOLD MADE IN U.S.A.".   **$20 - 25**

    3. White dustpan with blue trim and floral design, no markings.   **$5 - 10**

205

Miscellaneous

ROW 1:

    1. Pink and green toothbrush holder, marked with a black ink   **$30 - 40**
stamp "TULIP TOOTHBRUSH HOLDER © Artists' Barn Fillmore,
Calif. Use nail in each hole".

    2. Pink and green match holder, marked with a black ink stamp   **$20 - 25**
"TULIP MATCH HOLDER © Artists' Barn Fillmore, Calif.".
Original selling price is on the back 89¢.

    3. Toothbrush holder, a man peeking over the fence, mark is incised   **$60 - 70**
"RG.". This piece was sold new in 1950 at the Woolworth Dime
Store, Commercial Street, Springfield, MO.

ROW 2:

    1. Toothpick or match holder, made of real shells, marked with   **$50 - 60**
a black ink stamp "WORLDS FAIR ST. LOUIS, 1904".

    2. White toothpick holder with dogwood blossoms, no markings.   **$10 - 15**

ROW 3:

    1. Teapot string holder, white decorated with colorful roosters. The   **$60 - 70**
string comes out of the spout, marked with a blue paper label
"FREDROBERTS COMPANY. SAN FRANCISCO. MADE IN JAPAN".

    2. Love birds string holder, no markings. Made by Morton Pottery,   **$60 - 70**
Morton, Illinois, catalog #443.

    3. A yellow and white bird house, marked on the front in black letters   **$25 - 30**
"FOR WREN-T", and also incised on the back "PAT. PENDING".

ROW 4:

A pair of green holders, one with a black cat and one with a white cat.
Both are marked the same with a paper label that reads "Sheila
PLAQUE HANGERS For CUPS or POT HOLDERS. MOST ATTRACTIVE
WHEN HUNG IN PAIRS. demaree MOLDED PLASTICS KOKOMO,
INDIANA. 29¢".

Price per pair – $25 - 35

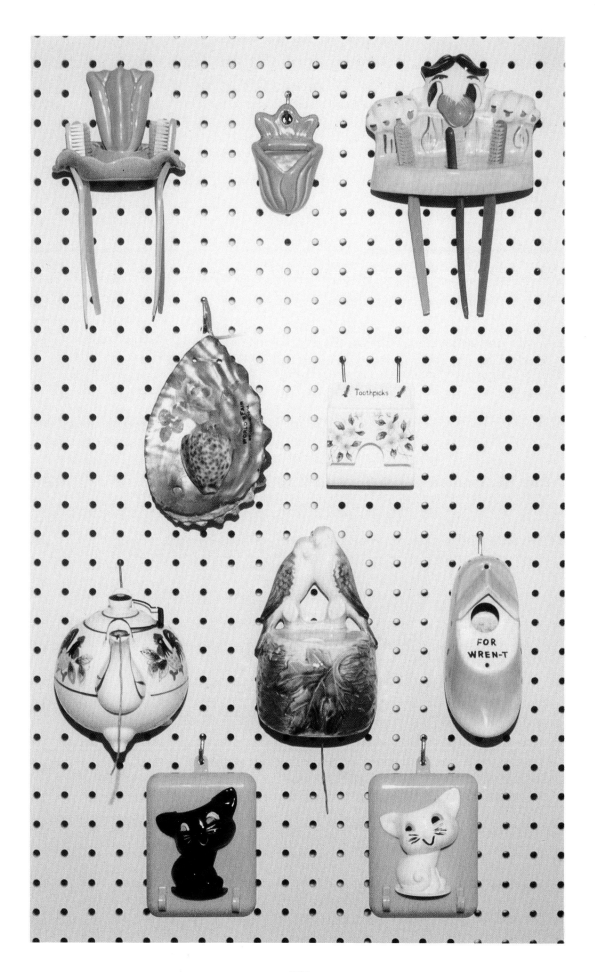

Miscellaneous

ROW 1:

    1. Little red riding hood toothbrush holder, mark incised "MADE IN JAPAN".   **$75 - 100**

    2. Black mule weather forecaster, marked on bottom with a black ink stamp "MADE IN JAPAN". Marked on front in gold letters "Instructions: **$25 - 30**

            If tail is dry – Fine
            If tail is wet – Rain
            If tail moves – Windy
            If tail cannot be seen – Fog
            If tail is frozen – Cold
            If tail falls out – Earthquake".

    3. White and red teapot with the Eastern Star emblem on the lid. Marked on the front in black "I'LL HOLD YOUR RINGS FOR YOU WHILE DISHES OR WASHING YOU DO". This piece is made of wood.   **$15 - 20**

ROW 2:

    1. Blue dog toothbrush holder, marked with a red ink stamp "GOLDCASTLE HAND-PAINTED CHIKUSA MADE IN JAPAN".   **$60 - 70**

    2. Two sailor boys with an anchor toothbrush holder, marked with a red ink stamp "MADE IN JAPAN", and also incised "JAPAN".   **$60 - 70**

ROW 3:

    1. Wood match holder with a Dutch scene, marked on front "MATCHES" and "COLUMBIA, MO.".   **$15 - 20**

    2. Blond girl toothbrush holder, mark incised "© G.B. CORP.", and also marked with a black ink stamp "MADE IN JAPAN".   **$60 - 70**

    3. Green clown bank, marked with a black ink stamp "Empire Savings DENVER COLORADO COORS". Made by Coors Porcelain Company, Golden, Colorado.   **$100 - 125**

ROW 4:

    Blue pig bank, no markings, made by Morton Pottery Company, Morton, Illinois. This pig is named "SKEDADDLE", catalog #671.   **$40 - 50**

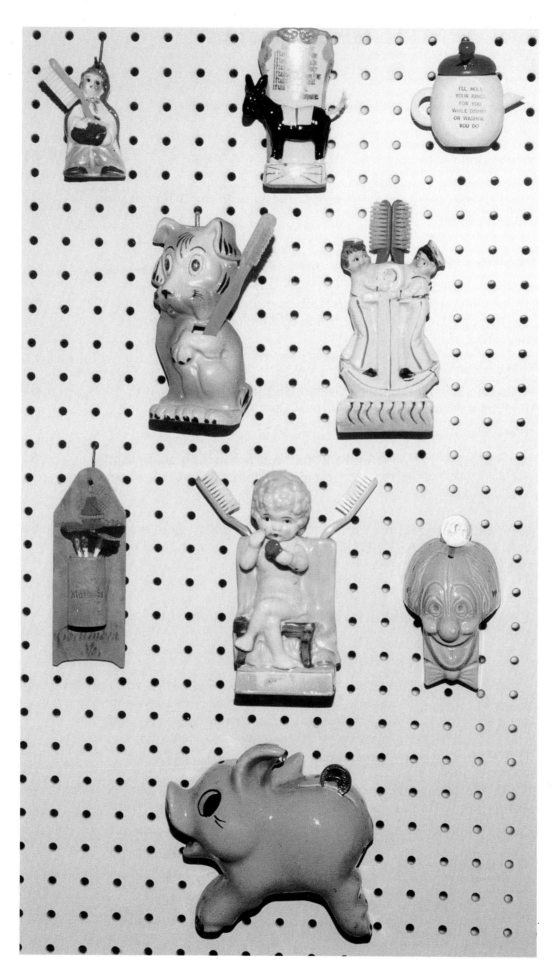

Miscellaneous

ROW 1:

1. Yellow violin with gold trim, 7$1/2$" tall, no markings.   **$15 - 20**

2. White violin with gold trim, 3$1/8$" tall, no markings.   **$15 - 20**

   The two above are from different patterns, and are different than the four below.

ROW 2:

1. White violin with gold trim, 8" tall, marked with a gold stamp "WARRANTED 22 K GOLD". Made by Morton Pottery Co., Morton, IL.   **$15 - 20**

2. White violin with floral decals and gold trim, 9$1/8$" tall, no markings. Made by Morton Pottery Co., Morton, Illinois.   **$20 - 25**

3. Rose violin with gold trim, 8$3/4$" tall, marked with a gold stamp "GOLDRA E. PALESTINE O.". Made by Goldra, East Palestine, Ohio.   **$15 - 20**

4. Tan violin with gold trim, 8$1/2$" tall, marked with a gold stamp "GOLDRA E. PALESTINE O.". (Same as #3), with original price 69¢.   **$15 - 20**

ROW 3:

1 & 2. A pair of white and blue floral decals, no markings, used as humidifiers.   Priced per pair – **$40 - 55**

3. Back view of humidifier pockets. The back side is not glazed and the finish is rough, porous and has grooves for water evaporation. They hang by a hook on a metal hot water heat radiator to put moisture into the air. These are used for this purpose in Germany.

4 & 5. A pair of white pockets with brown flowers and cattails, no markings, same rough grooves, used as humidifiers.   **$40 - 55**

NOTE:
All the above pockets in row three can also be used as wall pockets for flowers.

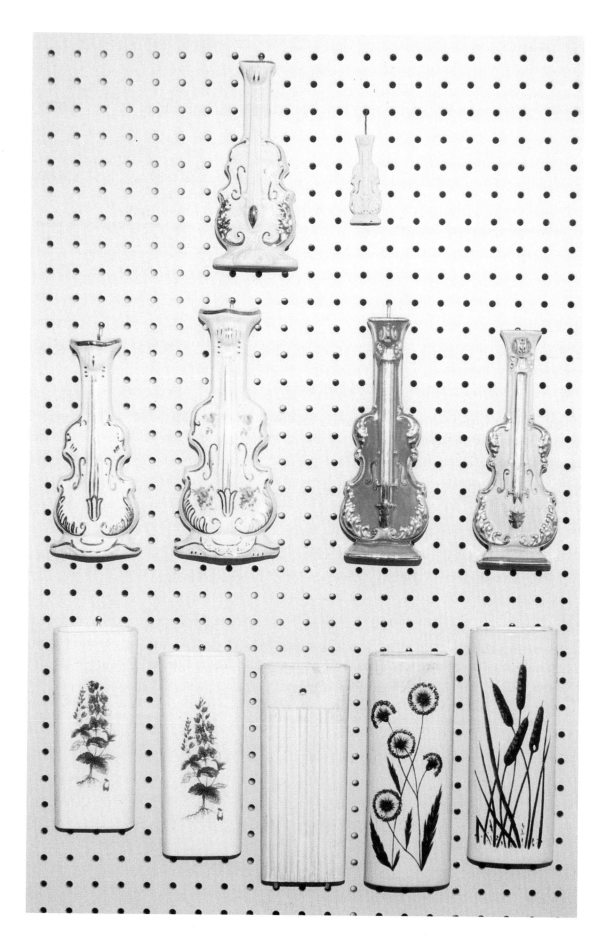

Miscellaneous

ROW 1:

    1. Green Indonesian head with a fancy headdress, no markings.   **$25 - 30**

    2. A young lad dressed in a white cap and shirt decorated with   **$40 - 50**
red polka dots, no markings. In our first book we show a boy
called "Sandy" that is very similar to this boy, but the hair, hat,
clothes and base are different.

ROW 2:

    1. Lady's head wearing a green hat, no markings.   **$20 - 25**

    2. A woman with brown hair, wearing earrings and a black   **$15 - 20**
necklace, no markings.

ROW 3:

    1. Petite blonde lady dressed in black, no markings. This wall   **$25 - 30**
pocket is similar to the head vases a lot of people collect.

    2. A young girl wearing a black hat, decorated with flowers and a   **$20 - 25**
plaid bow, no markings. This wall pocket most likely had a
boy opposite the girl and came as a set.

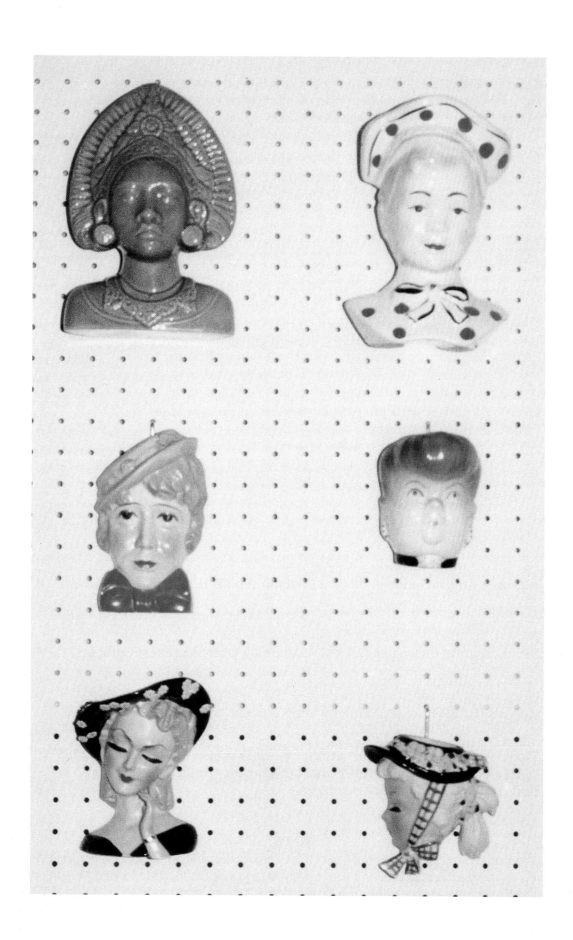

Miscellaneous

ROW 1:

1. Vase type wall pocket with a large pink flower, trimmed with gold,   **$25 - 30**
no markings. Identified as made by American Pottery Company,
of Marietta and Byesville, Ohio.

2. Blue wall pocket with a blue bird and leaves, no markings. This type   **$15 - 20**
was made to hang on a wall, in a corner, or to sit as a vase. Made
by Ohio Porcelain Company, Zanesville, Ohio, 1940-1956.

3. Heart with blue bow, gold trim, marked "USA". Made by   **$30 - 35**
American Pottery Co.

The American Pottery Company began producing in 1942 and continuing
until 1965 when it closed. Many of us confuse it with The American
Bisque Pottery, since their pieces look a lot alike. They were two different
potteries with the same owners. American Bisque produced until 1982.

ROW 2:

1. Blue wall pocket with purple flowers, no markings. Made by   **$15 - 20**
Ohio Porcelain Company.

2. Green triple wall pocket with purple flowers, no markings. Made   **$15 - 20**
by Ohio Porcelain Company.

3. Yellow, no markings, same as #1.   **$15 - 20**

ROW 3:   All three are the same style, see information on Row 1, No. 2.   each – **$15 - 20**

ROW 4:

1. Head, mark is incised "© O.P.CO.". Made by Ohio Porcelain Company.   **$30 - 40**

2. Tray, duck/cattails, mark is incised "PAT-PENDING O.P.CO.   **$10 - 15**
ZANESVILLE O. USA". Made by Ohio Porcelain Co.

3. Three wall pockets, ducks/cattails, mark is incised "PATENTED
149144". Made by Ohio Porcelain Co. These were also made as an
opposite pair and in various colors.   each – **$15 - 25**

NOTE:
*We have seen pieces with the O.P.CO. mark identified as Owen Pottery Co.
by some dealers, according to Kovel's Antique & Collectibles Price Guide
1996, Owens Pottery only made art pottery from 1896 to 1907.*

215

Miscellaneous

ROW 1:

    1. Black "Bully", bulls head, no markings, maker unknown.   **$25 - 30**

    2. Squirrel, mark is incised "USA 234-F", maker unknown. This   **$75 - 85**
       is an extra nice piece with a very soft satin glaze. It was made
       to hang or sit as a vase.

    3. Black scotty dog head, extra heavy, no markings, maker unknown.   **$30 - 40**

ROW 2:

    1. Electric lamp wall pocket, shaped like an old stove, the design   **$25 - 35**
       on the shade matches design of stove. The stove wall pocket
       is not marked.

    2. Stove wall pocket, less the metal bracket and other accessories   **$15 - 20**
       that would make it into a lamp. This piece has an incised
       mark "USA", maker unknown.

    3. A pair of bamboo pockets, no markings, maker unknown.   Price each – **$15 - 20**
       These have two compartments in each piece, one in the top
       and one in the bottom. It has a partition in the middle.

ROW 3:

    1. Dumbo and mouse, mark is incised "© DUMBO WALT DISNEY   **$100 - 125**
       PROD."

    2. Pluto and cart, mark is incised "© PLUTO WALT DISNEY PROD.".   **$100 - 125**

    3. Bambi and Thumper, mark is incised "© BAMBI WALT DISNEY   **$100 - 125**
       PROD."

NOTES:

*The Walt Disney wall pockets were made for the Leeds China Company,
Chicago, Illinois, (a distributor), by one of several different potteries.
Ludowici Celedon, American Bisque, American Pottery and others are
known to have made pieces for Leeds China Company, so we can
not positively identify the maker of these wall pockets. We think these
wall pockets are very unique because they can be collected for their
appeal as wall pockets or as Walt Disney memorabilia. We hope to
find others in this series.*

MISCELLANEOUS – LATE COMERS

The wall pockets on this page and the following pages in this chapter are pictures that came in late. We wanted to include them, so we are putting them here and are identifying the ones we can for you.

ROW 1:

    1. White ladies hat, multicolored flowers, mark is incised "*Weil* Ware",   **$40 - 50**
and also marked with a black ink stamp "1039".

    2. Lady in a red dress, with gold trim, mark is impressed   **$100 - 125**
"GERMANY 3817".

ROW 2:

    1. Heart shape, multicolored design, mark is incised "KERALIT   **$30 - 40**
58 B". Made in Germany.

    2. Basket with flowers and trimmed with gold, no markings.   **$30 - 40**

    3. Food grinder with cherry, no markings, made in California.   **$25 - 30**

ROW 3:

    1. White harp with gold trim, no markings.   **$25 - 30**

    2. Skillet with cherries, no markings, made in California.   **$25 - 30**

    3. Brown violin, no markings.   **$20 - 30**

ROW 4:

    A white rolling pin with red trim, marked with raised letters   **$25 - 30**
"HYALYN 510". This piece was made by Hyalyn Porcelain, of
Hickory, North Carolina. It started in 1947 by two potters from
Zanesville, Ohio and is known to make kitchen items and planters.

219

Miscellaneous – late comers

ROW 1:

1. Red top, mark is incised "12451". (Looks like Germany porcelain and numbers).   **$40 - 50**

2. Yellow ladies hat with green bow, no markings.   **$30 - 40**

3. Dark blue and has a shield like a coat of arms, no markings, Dryden Pottery made special pieces like this.   **$40 - 50**

ROW 2:

1. Dark blue luster finish, and has the design of tree limbs with oriental hanging lanterns, marked with a red ink stamp "HAND-PAINTED MADE IN JAPAN". This piece is exceptionally beautiful, one of the best we have seen. The dealers price on this is $225.00 firm.   **$175 - 225**

2. Wagon with fruit design, marked with a foil label that reads "Ucago CERAMICS JAPAN".   **$35 - 40**

3. Blue with a bird and an orange flower, moriage decor and gold trim, marked with a red ink stamp "MADE IN JAPAN".   **$75 - 85**

ROW 3:

1. Triple pocket, white with aqua blue and brown lines and dots, 8 1/2" tall, marked with a blue ink stamp "(Royal Crown) Germany".   **$40 - 50**

2. Light green arrowhead, mark is incised "CREEK (with a tepee)".   **$35 - 45**

3. Yellow luster with red trim and flowers, marked with a red ink stamp "GOLD CASTLE HAND-PAINTED CHIKUSA MADE IN JAPAN".   **$45 - 55**

ROW 4:

1. Dark green arrowhead, mark incised "CREEK (with a tepee)".   **$35 - 45**

2. Small Indian head on a hatchet, no markings, made in Japan.   **$20 - 25**

3. Dark green arrowhead, mark incised "CREEK (with a tepee)".   **$35 - 45**

The arrowheads on this page were made at the Creek Pottery in Checotah, Oklahoma by the Creek Indians. This pottery was started in 1970 and closed in 1976.

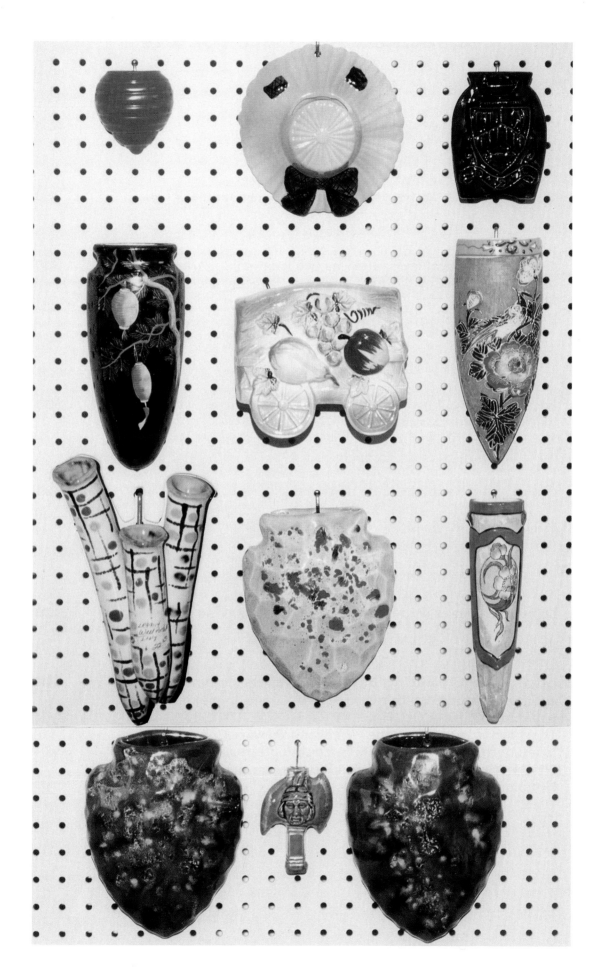

Miscellaneous – late comers

ROW 1:

    1. Chef with a yellow cap, no markings.   **$25 - 30**

    2. Blue grapes with leaves, extra nice and heavy, no markings.   **$30 - 40**

    3. Green with vertical lines, and has two long mold marks on the back like the McCoy Mexican man and the Shawnee daffodil, no markings.   **$20 - 25**

ROW 2:

    1. Ivory colored wall pocket with vertical lines, marked with black ink stamp "Camark".   **$30 - 35**

    2. Guitar, mauve and black, no markings.   **$25 - 30**

ROW 3:

    1. Light green flower with brown trim, very delicate, no markings.   **$20 - 25**

    2. Large pink wall pocket with grapes and leaves design, extra nice and heavy, marked with raised letters "U.S.A.", and also has a paper label "MONMOUTH POTTERY, MONMOUTH, ILL. #440-0". This piece was made by the Western Stoneware Company, Monmouth, IL. 1906-1985. Monmouth Pottery merged with Western Stoneware in 1906 and Western continued using the Monmouth label.   **$40 - 60**

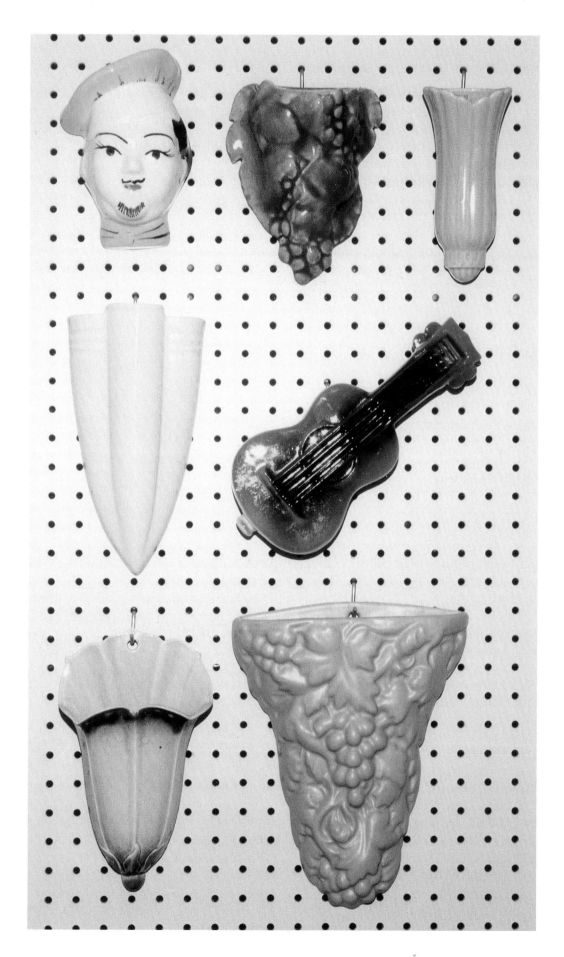

223

Miscellaneous – late comers

ROW 1:

1. A girl towel holder, no markings. This piece has two glass marbles in it's hand. In the back side is a small envelope that reads, "IMPORTANT –
(1) Place marbles in hand of "Grip-A-Towel" before mounting.
(2) Slip towel up into hand as far as possible.
(3) Do not pull too hard on towel".   **$25 - 30**

2. Clown scouring pad holder, no markings.   **$10 - 12**

3. A boy towel holder, same information as #1.   **$25 - 30**

Price per pair – **$55 - 65**

ROW 2:

1. Match box holder, mushrooms, no markings.   **$10 - 15**

2. Bath salts box with a wood scoop, marked with a paper label "BATH SALTS EARLY AMERICAN OLD SPICE REG & PAT'D". Original price tag on a back side $1.25.   **$25 - 35**

3. Match box holder, strawberries, mark is incised "McNEES Original M-677".   **$10 - 15**

ROW 3:

1. Salt and pepper wall holder, all three pieces are marked with a black ink stamp "JAPAN". The original price is on the bottom 59¢.   **$20 - 25**

2. Wood rolling pin holder (4 spice's) with copper metal rack, no markings.   **$15 - 20**

3. Salt and pepper wall holder, all three are marked with a black ink stamp "JAPAN 5B/701".   **$20 - 25**

ROW 4:

1. Green/pink tint butterfly, mark is incised "3532 California".   **$20 - 25**

2. Wood wall hanger, marked on front "CORNUCOPIA BRAND MIXED FRUIT-PACKED FOR APPLE CUPBOARD GROCERY CO. MEMPHIS TENNESSEE 1988 © TRADITIONS", and a foil label that reads "MADE IN TAIWAN R.O.C.".   **$3 - 7**

3. A butterfly, same as #1.   Price per pair – **$40 - 50**

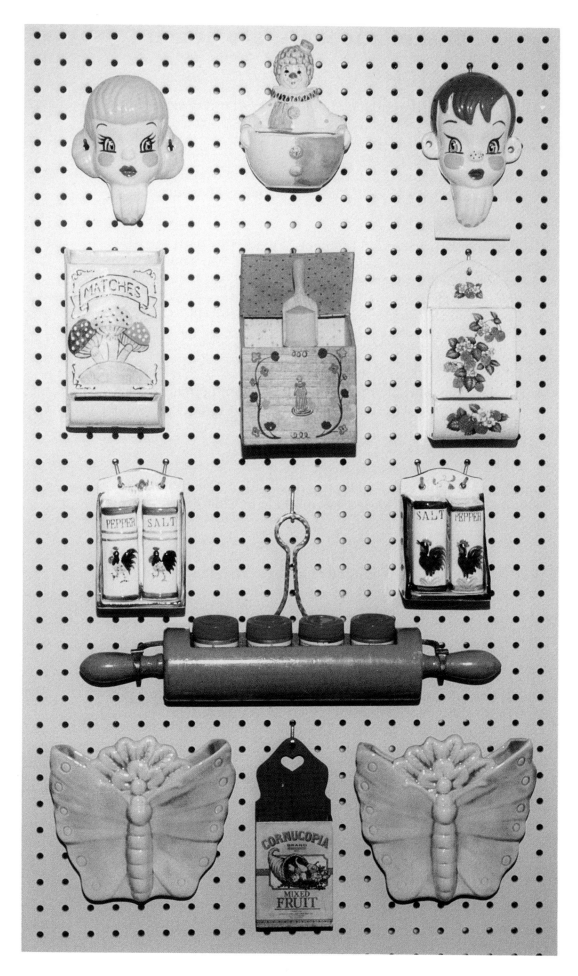

225

Miscellaneous – late comers

ROW 1:

1. Masonic emblem, handmade of black walnut and bird's-eye maple wood. The heart is hollow and open at the top. **$75 - 100**

2. Masonic emblem and dutch boy, handmade of wood, gold accent, 6" tall. From lodge #459 A.F. & A.M. Seymour, Missouri. **$35 - 50**

3. Back side of #1, written on the back "I made this with my pocket knife – T.W. Stevenson", and also a picture of "Mr. Thomas W. Stevenson, 1917, Lodge #43 A.F. and A.M., Bloomington, Illinois". This piece is 9 3/4" tall. We saw one other Masonic wall pocket at the Roy Rogers Museum, in Victorville, CA. **$75 - 100**

ROW 2:

A true opposite pair, pink and white, gold trim, no markings, 4" tall. Price per pair – **$50 - 65**

ROW 3:

1. Dutch woman, blue and white, marked with a black ink stamp "Hand Decorated Weil Ware (Burro) made in California", and also impressed "4078", 7" tall. **$35 - 40**

2. Blue metal holder, 8 1/2" tall, no markings. Probably an old car vase or used to hold flowers in a funeral hearse.

3. Glass insert for #2 metal holder, 7" tall. Price per set – **$125 - 175**

4. Dutch woman, yellow and white, marked only with an impressed "4078", 7" tall. Identified as Weil Ware, made by California Figurine Co., founded by Max Weil, 1940 until 1955. **$35 - 40**

ROW 4:

1. Electric clock/wall pocket, Dutch couple sitting, no markings, 12" tall. Marked by dealer on sale ticket as Hull Pottery, (could not verify). **$225 - 250**

2. Green with an iris flower, no markings, 6" tall. **$35 - 50**

3. Electric clock with wall pocket, with windmill and pair of Dutch kids, no markings, 11 1/2" tall. **$75 - 100**

Miscellaneous – late comers

ROW 1:

1. Little Orphan Annie with her dog, white with gold trim, 5 1/2" tall, marked with a red ink stamp "MADE IN JAPAN".   **$100 - 125**

2. Red cat woman with a real fur skirt, that has gold accents, the spear is missing, mark unknown, (Japan) 7 1/2" tall. Please look in our Japan Miscellaneous chapter for two other cat women in a black color.   **$30 - 40**

3. White chef sitting on a food grinder, no markings. Identified as "HOLLYWOOD CERAMICS" of Los Angeles, CA, 5 1/2" tall.   **$35 - 40**

4. Cherub on pink bisque, no markings, 6" tall.   **$35 - 40**

ROW 2:

1. Front and back view of a satin green shell, 6" tall, with an impressed mark "STANGL USA 3238".   **$100 - 125**

2. Bird, long tailed multicolored greens, marked "FULPER 375". size unknown, made by Fulper Pottery, Trenton, New Jersey.   **$275 - 300**

3. A pair of vegetable wall pockets, size and mark unknown, (Japan).   each – **$20 - 25**
Priced per pair – **$40 - 50**

ROW 3:

1. Blue and white falcon, 8 1/2" tall, this piece is extra heavy and no markings. It has the European look.   **$75 - 125**

2. Green and white falcon, 8 1/2" tall, this piece is similar to the blue falcon, but is finished in more detail.   **$75 - 125**

3. White heron, 5" tall, no markings, looks like Japan.   **$35 - 45**

4. Blue panels, 7 3/4" tall, mark impressed "MADE IN USA". The mark is inside an impressed acorn shape.   **$35 - 45**

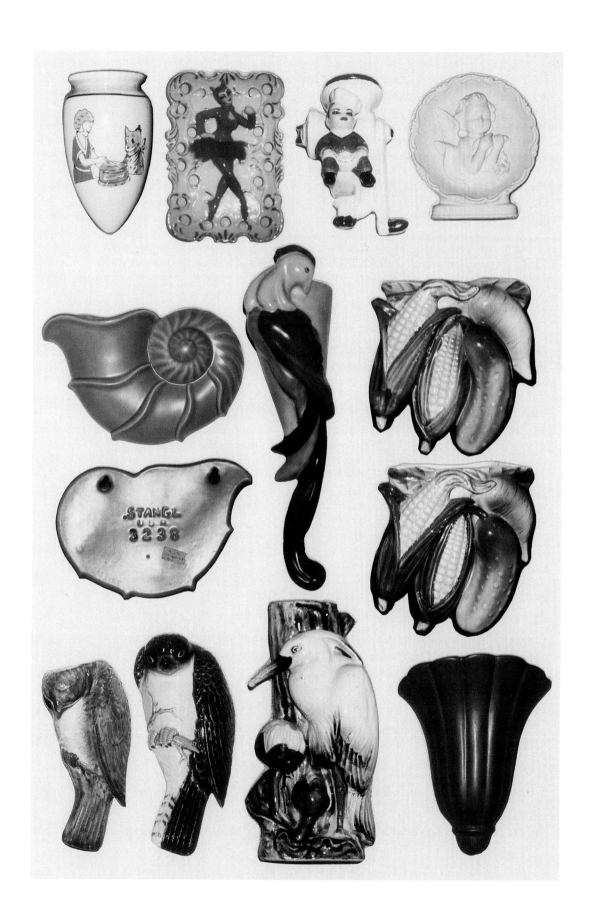

Miscellaneous – late comers

ROW 1:

1. Pair of wall pockets, boy and girl rabbits, plastic and hardboard, marked "MADE IN USA BURWOOD CO.", 6" tall.   **$10 - 15**

2. Porch pocket with Eagle, mark is incised on left side "ELLIS DAVIDSON CO.", and on the right side "New York City", 8 1/2" tall.   **$40 - 50**

3. Black and tan pocket, 10" tall, only mark is a blue line near the hole in the back.   **$60 - 70**

4. Pink flamingos, their necks are the handles, no markings, 7" tall.   **$40 - 50**

ROW 2:

1. Ladies hat, marked with a red ink stamp "51/132", and also has a silver foil label "Hand-painted MADE IN JAPAN THAMES".   **$30 - 35**

2. Tan and brown, ivy design, 8 1/2" tall, no markings, extra nice, unidentified.   **$60 - 70**

3. A pair of red plastic pots, marked with raised letters "Bernard Edward Co., Chicago USA", 11" tall.   **$15 - 20**

ROW 3:

1. A girl in a ring, marked with a black ink stamp "MADE IN JAPAN", and also incised "MD 716". This piece is 6 3/4" tall.   **$25 - 30**

2. Clown toothbrush holder, 5" tall, marked with a red ink stamp "MADE IN JAPAN".   **$60 - 75**

ROW 4:

1. Oriental woman, no markings, 9" tall.   **$40 - 50**

2. Hull, white oval frame (Athena), #611, 8 1/2" tall, mark unknown.   **$75 - 100**

3. Open rose (Camellia) #125, Hull, pink, 8 1/2" tall, mark unknown.   **$350 - 450**

4. Coat of Arms shield, marked with a black ink stamp "(Bird) W.H. GOSS". This was made by William Henry Goss, Stoke Staffordshire, England and is 2 1/2" tall.   **$40 - 50**

Miscellaneous – late comers

ROW 1:

1. Brown pocket, marked with a black ink stamp "SHONIER & SONS STOKE-ON TRENT ENGLAND", also incised "292", 8" tall.   **$75 - 85**

2. Flamingos with necks as handles, pinkish-brown color, no markings, 7" tall.   **$40 - 50**

3. Brown to pearl color, no markings, 81/2" tall. Identified as Peters and Reed, and has a 1/2" hole in the back for hanging.   **$100 - 125**

4. Native head, green with gold trim, no markings, 8" tall.   **$35 - 45**

ROW 2:

1. Clock/bird, marked with a red ink stamp "MADE IN OCCUPIED JAPAN", 23/8" tall. This is the smallest pocket we have ever seen.   **$25 - 35**

2. Willow pocket, no markings, 101/2" tall. This was made from willow sticks that were bent while the sticks were still green.   **$15 - 20**

3. Wood cigarette pack holder with rooster design, no markings, 11" tall. These were also made by other companies in ceramic and other materials.   **$30 - 40**

4. Hillbilly wall pocket, this was found in an old cabin back in the Ozark hills, it consists of an old metal lamp reflector, hand carved walnut bowl, two bullets, a screwdriver and held together with a wooden clothespin, 10" tall. This piece hangs above Marvin's desk. Priced without bullets and screwdriver.   **$10 - 15**

ROW 3:

1. Front and back view of a bag with applied hat, marked with a blue ink stamp "FULL BEE". Identified as a "Goebel", made in Germany 1950-1955, 5" tall.   **$60 - 80**

2. Yellow and green blossom, mark is incised "CASTOR BEAN CALIFORNIA ARTS", 71/2" tall.   **$25 - 30**

3. Front and back view of a baseball glove, mark incised "DON HEFFNER MONROVIA CALIF ©", 5" tall.   **$25 - 30**

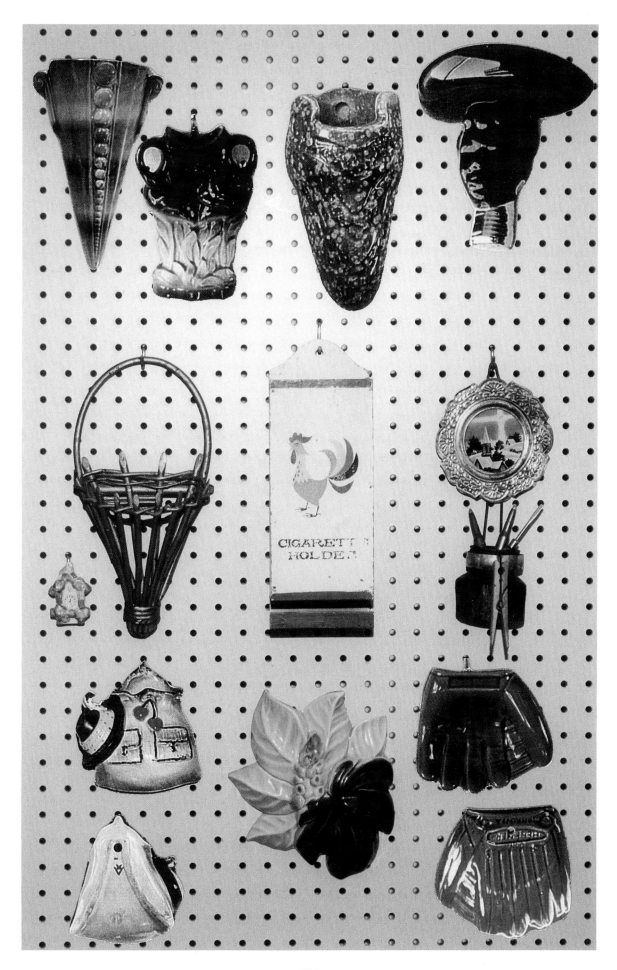

MORTON POTTERIES

Morton Pottery consisted of five different potteries that operated in Morton, Illinois over a period of 99 years, from 1877-1976. It all started with the six Rapp brothers from Burgberg, Germany in 1877 to 1936, then Morton Pottery 1922-1976, Cliffwood Art Pottery 1920-1940, Midwest Potteries, Inc. 1940-1944, American Art Pottery 1947-1963, with Morton Pottery running until it closed in 1976. The Rapp family was involved in all phases of the Morton, Illinois potteries.

ROW 1:

1. Red apple, no markings, made by American Art Pottery, Morton, Ill.   **$20 - 25**

2. Matte green corner, no markings, made by The Morton Pottery   **$50 - 60**
Company, Morton, IL.

3. Brown and yellow drip glaze, no markings, made by Midwest   **$20 - 25**
Potteries, Inc., Morton, IL.

ROW 2:

1. Yellow pig wall pocket, #671, no markings, legs spread, called   **$30 - 35**
"SKEDADDLE".

2. Green pig wall pocket, $672, no markings, legs together, called   **$30 - 35**
"SKEDOODLE".

3. Blue pig bank #671, no markings, legs spread, called "SKEDADDLE".   **$40 - 50**
All pigs made by Morton Pottery Company.

ROW 3:

1. Lady with hat, no markings, made by Morton Pottery Co., Morton, IL.   **$50 - 60**

2. White moon basket, no markings, will hang or sit as a vase.   **$40 - 50**
This piece was on the cover of a "Rapp Artcraft Pottery" catalog,
Morton, Illinois.

NOTE:
The following are other Morton wall pockets known to us, but not in either of our two books.
1. Vase type #123, made in 6" and 8 3/4" sizes.
2. Tree trunk with three limb openings, 8" tall.
3. Vase type with handles, soft matte glaze, 7 1/2" tall.
(Above three made by Cliftwood Art Pottery, Morton, IL)
4. Tree stump with applied bird, 5" tall.
5. Chrysanthemum flower, 8" tall.
(Above two made by Midwest Potteries, Inc., Morton, IL)
6. Head vase wall pocket (Betty Grable type) cold painted.
7. Fish wall pocket, used as a jewelry holder.
(Above two made by Morton Pottery Co., Morton IL).

Morton Potteries

ROW 1:

    1. Blue scoop, no markings, made by Morton Pottery Co., Morton, IL.   **$15 - 20**

    2. Lady with a hoe, no markings, made by Morton Pottery Co., Morton, IL.   **$35 - 40**

    3. Green wishing well, gold trim, no markings, Morton Pottery Co., Morton, IL.   **$15 - 20**

ROW 2:

    1. Pink iron, no markings, made by Morton Pottery Co., Morton, IL.   **$20 - 25**

    2. White teapot, no markings, made by Morton Pottery Co., Morton, IL.   **$15 - 20**

ROW 3:

    1. Pink embossed diamond weave with flared shape, #644, no markings, made in 1951, Morton Pottery Co.   **$15 - 20**

    2. Mulberry color #123, no markings, made by Cliftwood Art Pottery, Morton, IL.   **$40 - 50**

    3. Blue ribbed, no markings, made by Cliftwood Art Pottery, Morton, IL.   **$40 - 50**

NOTE:

The following wall pockets are shown in our first book.

1. Bird house with birds #485.
2. Bird with head down #643.
3. Bird with head up #700
4. Chickens, hen or rooster, no numbers.
5. Cockatiels #424 and #578.
6. Corner wall pocket, no number.
7. Lady watering flowers #445.
8. Lattice with flower pot #467.
9. Open lattice with flower pot, no number.
10. Love birds #443.
11. Owl on quarter moon, no number.
12. Parrot with grapes, no number.
13. Peacock #684.
14. Vase type with floral design, 6" tall, no number.

None of the above are marked.

237

PETERS AND REED POTTERY

John Peters and Adam Reed were working for the Weller Pottery, in Putnam, Ohio, when they decided to start a pottery of their own in Zanesville, Ohio, it operated from 1897 to 1921, when it became Zane Pottery and changed names again in 1941 to Gonder Pottery. It closed permanently in 1957.

ROW 1:

    1. Peters and Reed, matte green over red clay, embossed top border,   **$100 - 125**
no markings, but has a 1/2" hole in the back for hanging.

    2. Peters and Reed, matte cream over red clay, "EGYPTIAN WARE",   **$100 - 125**
profile of an Egyptian Pharaoh, no markings, 5/8" hole.

ROW 2:

    1. Peters and Reed, "VELTON WARE", this has a pink luster like   **$100 - 125**
finish over grey and white, and has a 1/2" hole in the back.

    2. Peters and Reed, brown, "MOSS AZTEC", grapes and leaves,   **$100 - 125**
and has a 1/2" hole.

NOTE:
Peters and Reed pottery is not marked, but the one thing all of these have in common is a very large hole for hanging and the three ground firing prongs on the back.

RED WING POTTERY

Red Wing Pottery began in Red Wing, Minnesota in 1878, making utilitarian pottery. They started making art pottery in the 1920's. The company closed in 1967, but the old pottery is still a tourist attraction with many visitors each year.

ROW 3:

    1. Cornucopia, aqua, mark is incised "RED WING 441".   **$40 - 50**

    2. Green wall pocket, marked with raised letters "RED WING U.S.A.   **$30 - 40**
M-1629".

ROW 4:

    1. Violin, brown, marked with raised letters "RED WING U.S.A. 907".   **$30 - 40**

    2. Cornucopia, pink, mark is incised "RED WING 441".   **$40 - 50**

    3. Mandolin, black, marked with raised letters "RED WING U.S.A.   **$35 - 45**
M-1484", and it also has a red and gold paper label "ART POTTERY".

239

Red Wing Pottery

ROW 1:

    1. Violin, rust color, marked with raised letters "RED WING **$30 - 40**
U.S.A. 907".

    2. Mandolin, aqua color, marked with raised letters "RED **$30 - 40**
WING U.S.A. M-1484".

    3. White with flower design and orange highlights, mark is **$75 - 90**
incised "RED WING U.S.A. 1231".

ROW 2:

    White shell design, mark is incised "RED WING U.S.A. 1254". **$40 - 50**
The inside of this piece has a glossy green glaze.

ROW 3:

    Fancy pocket with pink speckled color, mark is incised "RED **$75 - 90**
WING U.S.A. M-1517.

NOTE:

Red Wing Pottery began as the Red Wing Stoneware Company in Red Wing, Minnesota in 1878, changing it's name to the Red Wing Union Stoneware Company in 1906. In 1936 it was changed for the last time to Red Wing Potteries, Inc. The company made stoneware crocks, jars and jugs in the early years. About 1920 the company began making vases, cookie jars and other art pottery. In the 1930's Red Wing produced pottery for George Rumrill along with a large line of dinnerware. The 1920's through the 1940's were very prosperous for Red Wing, but as it was for many of our U.S. potteries, foreign trade took it's toll on Red Wing Pottery and although they sought new markets and managed to get by for a few years, they finally closed in 1967.

241

ROOKWOOD POTTERY

Rookwood Pottery began in Cincinnati, Ohio in 1880 and continued until 1967. After 1900 most of their pieces were marked and dated. The name and some of the molds were sold in 1984, and a few new pieces were made, but these were glazed in colors not used by the original company.

ROW 1:

1. Rookwood, pink and green, mark is impressed "2008" and "Flame Mark", made in 1930.   **$175 - 250**

2. Rookwood, green, marked impressed "2940" and "Flame Mark" made in 1928.   **$175 - 250**

3. Rookwood, purple, mark impressed "2008" and "Flame Mark" made in 1930.   **$175 - 250**

ROW 2:

1. Rookwood, pink and green, mark impressed "2957" and "Flame Mark", made in 1927.   **$200 - 275**

2. Rookwood, yellow, mark impressed "2957" and "Flame Mark", made in 1926.   **$200 - 275**

ROSEMEADE POTTERY

Rosemeade Pottery (Wahpeton Pottery) of Wahpeton, North Dakota began in 1940 and continued production until 1961, using many wildlife designs in making wall pockets, salt and pepper shakers, figurines and other quality items. Rosemeade pottery is usually easy to recognize by their outstanding colors and glazes.

ROW 3:

1. Rosemeade, leaves, ivory and pink, marked with a blue ink stamp "Rosemeade".   **$50 - 75**

2. Rosemeade, half moon, tan and pink, marked with a blue ink stamp "Rosemeade".   **$40 - 60**

3. Rosemeade, leaves, ivory and pink, marked with a blue ink stamp "Rosemeade".   **$50 - 75**
Price per pair – **$100 - 150**

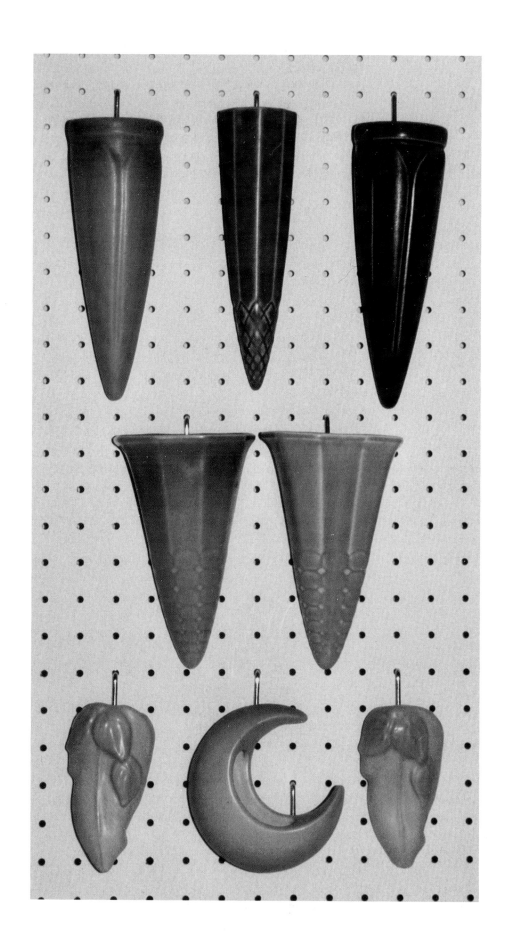

ROSEVILLE POTTERY

Roseville Pottery went into business in 1890, but did not start making art pottery until 1900, when Ross C. Purdy designed the "Rozane" pattern. Roseville Pottery went on to produce some of the most popular art pottery found today. It is almost impossible to put a price on Roseville wall pockets, because some collectors will pay much more than book price for one they want. So remember, the prices are only a guide in this book and especially in the Roseville chapter.

ROW 1:

    1. Green tint pattern, ivory and light green color, circa 1916, unmarked.   **$225 - 275**

    2. Corinthian Pattern, ivory and green color, circa 1923, unmarked.   **$175 - 225**

ROW 2:

    1. Moss pattern, green and rose color, circa 1930, mark is impressed "Roseville U.S.A. 1279".   **$400 - 500**

ROW 3:

    1. Dahlrose pattern, brown and green color, circa 1924, unmarked.   **$150 - 200**

    2. Velmoss scroll pattern, ivory and green color, circa 1916, marked with a paper label "ROSEVILLE POTTERY".   **$150 - 200**

NOTE:

Roseville collectors use the words "in relief" for the marks on Roseville pottery that have raised letters. The marks that are in relief are usually in script "Roseville".

Marks that are impressed are usually in capital letters "ROSEVILLE".

The ink stamp marks are usually in blue ink and fancy scroll letters "Rv".

Many pieces of Roseville pottery were marked with only paper labels. These came off or were taken off over the years, which make it very difficult for the ones that do not know Roseville pottery very well to identify some of the Roseville pieces.

Roseville Pottery

ROW 1:

1. Carnelian II pattern, brown and green color, circa 1915, marked with a blue ink stamp "Rv".   **$150 - 200**

2. Rosecraft Panel pattern, brown and green, circa 1920, marked with a blue ink stamp "Rv". The embossed design on this piece looks like a pumpkin vine, with five petal blossoms, leaves and small orange fruit. This design is also on the "BANEDA" pattern, circa 1933. Sometimes called the "LOVE APPLE" pattern. Another color variation will be shown later in this chapter.   **$225 - 275**

ROW 2:

LaRose pattern, ivory and green color, circa 1924, marked with a blue ink stamp "Rv".   **$200 - 250**

ROW 3:

1. Carnelian I pattern, brown and green color, circa 1910, marked with a blue ink stamp "Rv".   **$150 - 200**

2. Tuscany pattern, pink color, circa 1927, unmarked.   **$150 - 200**

NOTE:

To our knowledge there are approximately 135 Roseville wall pockets in different patterns, sizes or colors to be found.

The following is the list of <u>patterns</u> known to us.

Antique Matte, Apple Blossom, Baneda, Bittersweet, Blackberry, Bleeding Heart, Bordeaux Gardens, Burmese, Bushberry, Capri, Carnelian, Ceramic Design (White and Gold/Gold Traced/Decorated/Decorated Persian), Cherry Blossom, Chloron, Clematis, Columbine, Corinthian, Cosmos, Dahlrose, Dogwood, Donatello, Earlam, Ferella, Florane, Florentine, Foxglove, Freesia, Fuschia, Futura, Gardinia, Green Tint, Imperial, Iris, Ivory, Ivory Tint, Jonquil, Landscape, La Rose, Lombardy, Lotus, Luffa, Magnolia, Matte Green, Mayfair, Ming Tree, Morning Glory, Moss, Mostique, Orian, Panel, Peony, Persian, Pine Cone, Pink Tint, Poppy, Primrose, Rosecraft (Hexagon/Panel/Vintage), Royal Capri, Rozane, Savona, Silhouette, Snowberry, Sunflower, Thornapple, Tuscany, Velmoss, Velmoss Scroll, Vista, Volpato, White Rose, Wincraft, Wisteria, Yellow Tint, Zephyr Lily.

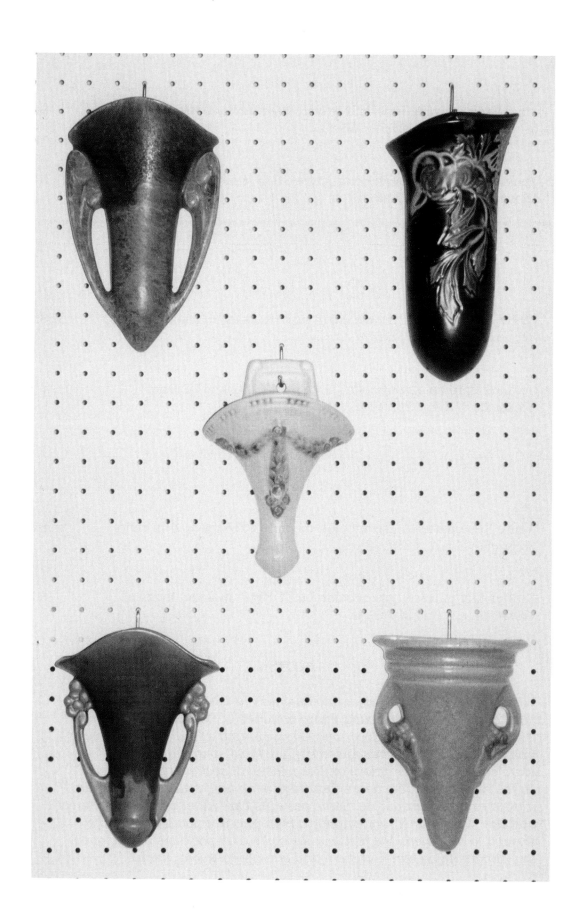

247

Roseville Pottery

ROW 1:

    1. Ming Tree pattern, blue and brown color, circa 1949, marked   **$250 - 300**
in relief "*Roseville U.S.A. 566-8*".

    2. Magnolia pattern, green color, circa 1943, marked in relief   **$175 - 225**
"*Roseville U.S.A. 1294-81/2*".

ROW 2:

    1. White Rose pattern, brown color, circa 1940's, marked in relief   **$200 - 250**
"*Roseville U.S.A. 1288-61/2*".

    2. Cosmos pattern, green color, circa 1940, marked in relief   **$150 - 200**
"*Roseville U.S.A. 1285-61/2*".

ROW 3:

    1. White Rose pattern, green color, circa 1940's, marked in relief   **$200 - 250**
"*Roseville U.S.A. 1289 - 81/2*".

    2. Zephyr Lily pattern, green color, circa 1946, marked in relief   **$150 - 200**
"*Roseville U.S.A. 1297-8*".

NOTE:

When Roseville Pottery went into business in 1890, times were very hard and there were already many potteries in Rosevillle, Ohio. But the Roseville Pottery thrived with George Young at the helm and went from making utility wares to some of the most sought after art ware of our time. The prices on Roseville wall pockets have changed so fast in the past few years that there is no way anyone can predict a price at an accurate rate. Some patterns like "Blackberry", "Sunflower", and the "Nude Panel" are extremely high priced-if you are fortunate enough to find them. We feel any Roseville wall pocket is a very good investment if you can find them and can afford to buy them.

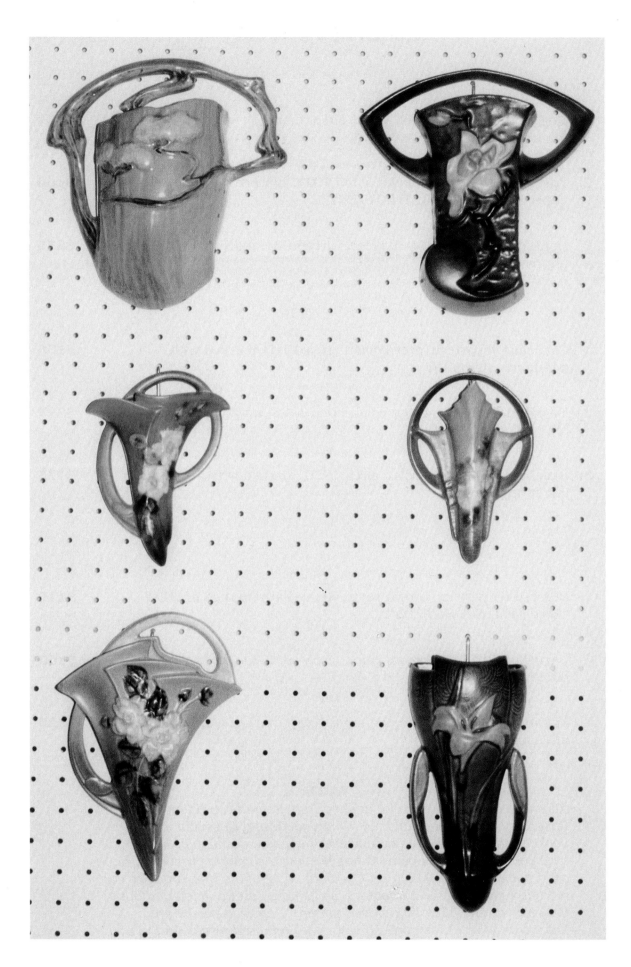

Roseville Pottery

1. Dogwood I pattern, green, circa 1918, marked with a blue   **$200 - 250**
   ink stamp "*Rv*".

2. Tuscany pattern, pink color, circa 1927, marked with a black   **$150 - 200**
   paper label "ROSEVILLE POTTERY".

3. Double pine cone pattern, green, circa 1931, mark is   **$250 - 300**
   impressed "ROSEVILLE 1273-8".

ROW 2:

1. Carnelian II pattern, green color, circa 1915, marked with   **$150 - 200**
   a blue ink stamp "*Rv*".

2. Dogwood II pattern, green color, circa 1928, marked with a   **$225 - 275**
   blue ink stamp "*Rv*".

3. Panel pattern, brown color, circa 1920, marked with a blue   **$175 - 225**
   ink stamp "*Rv*".

ROW 3:

1. Bittersweet pattern, brown color, circa 1940, marked in relief   **$125 - 175**
   "*Roseville U.S.A. 866-7$1/2$*".

2. Carnelian I pattern, brown color, circa 1910, marked with a   **$150 - 200**
   blue ink stamp "*Rv*".

3. Florane Pattern, brown color, circa 1920, marked with a blue   **$125 - 175**
   ink stamp "*Rv*".

NOTE:

All prices in this book are for wall pockets in mint condition. A Roseville collector once told me "When you buy a Roseville wall pocket with damage, all you will ever have is a damaged Roseville wall pocket". In recent years it has become a common practice to have good pottery repaired by a professional. Most of the time a novice can not tell a piece has been repaired, so be very careful when you buy Roseville or any other high priced pottery. Repaired pieces are not worth as much as mint, so if you buy repaired pieces and plan to resell them, you may not get a good return on your money.

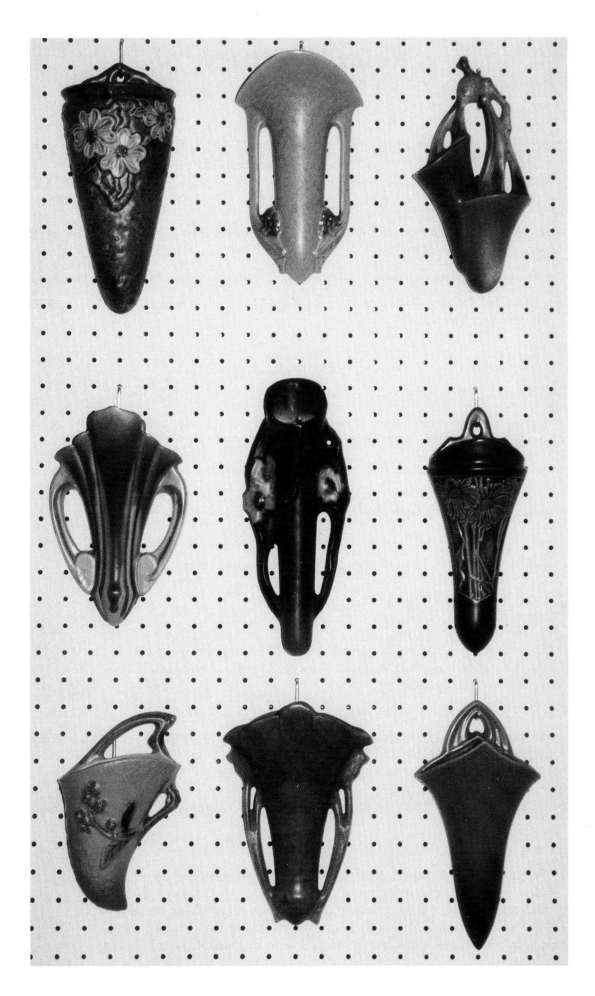

Roseville Pottery

ROW 1:

1. Carnelian I pattern, blue, circa 1910, marked with a blue ink
   stamp "Rv", and it also has a black paper label that reads
   "ROSEVILLE POTTERY".   **$150 - 200**

2. Magnolia pattern, brown color, circa 1943, marked in relief
   "Roseville U.S.A. 1294".   **$175 - 225**

3. Silhouette pattern, blue color, circa 1952, marked in relief
   "Roseville U.S.A. 766-8".   **$200 - 250**

ROW 2:

1. Rozane pattern, ivory with flowers, circa 1917, marked with a
   black ink stamp "ROSEVILLE ROZANE POTTERY".   **$150 - 200**

2. Donatello pattern, ivory, tan and green, circa 1915, marked
   with an impressed seal "DONATELLO RPCO".   **$200 - 250**

3. Dahlrose pattern, brown color, circa 1924, unmarked.   **$150 - 200**

ROW 3:

1. Matte green pocket, made before 1916. Most are not marked,
   but this piece has "four numbers" incised on the back that
   are impossible to read.   **$225 - 275**

2. Mayfair pattern, corner pocket, tan color, circa late 1940's,
   marked in relief *"Roseville U.S.A. 1014-8"*.   **$150 - 200**

3. Velmoss Scroll pattern, ivory color, circa 1916, unmarked. **$200 - 250**

NOTE:

*The more we dig into the history of Roseville pottery, the more
fascinated we become with it. Its a pottery that got started later
than some of the others in making art pottery, like Weller Pottery,
Owens Pottery and Rookwood Pottery, but became a front runner
in production and style very quickly and to this day is number one
in popularity.*

Roseville Pottery

ROW 1:

    1. Freesia pattern, brown color, circa 1945, marked in relief   **$175 - 225**
       "*Roseville U.S.A. 1296-8*".

    2. Rosecraft Panel (Nude) pattern, brown color, circa 1920-1924,   **$500 - 600**
       marked with a blue ink stamp "*Rv*".

    3. Freesia pattern, green in color, circa 1945, marked in relief   **$175 - 225**
       "*Roseville U.S.A. 1296-8*".

ROW 2:

    1. Clematis pattern, green in color, circa 1944, marked in relief   **$175 - 225**
       "*Roseville U.S.A. 1295-8*".

    2. Rosecraft Panel (Pumpkin/Love Apple) pattern, brown color,   **$175 - 225**
       circa 1920-1924, marked with a blue ink stamp "*Rv*", see note.

    3. Clematis pattern, brown color, circa 1944, marked in relief   **$175 - 225**
       "*Roseville U.S.A. 1295-8*".

ROW 3:

    1. Zephyr Lily pattern, brown color, circa 1946, marked in relief   **$200 - 250**
       "*Roseville U.S.A. 1297-8*".

    2. Double Dogwood II pattern, green color, circa 1928, unmarked.   **$200 - 250**

    3. Zephyr Lily pattern, blue color, circa 1946, marked in relief   **$200 - 250**
       "*Roseville U.S.A. 1297-8*".

NOTE:

*This Rosecraft Panel (Pumpkin/Love Apple) pattern was shown earlier
in this chapter in another color variation. The other piece definitely has
green leaves where this one does not. The other thing I found in my
personal research on the Rosecraft Panels, is the leaves in the designs
do not match the types of plants or flowers. The same shapes of leaves
were used on two different "Panel" pockets. I am not trying to be critical,
I'm an amateur artist and I love the designers' freedom to express their
own ideas. If I had the chance to design items and I liked a certain
shape of leaf, I would use it on everything.*

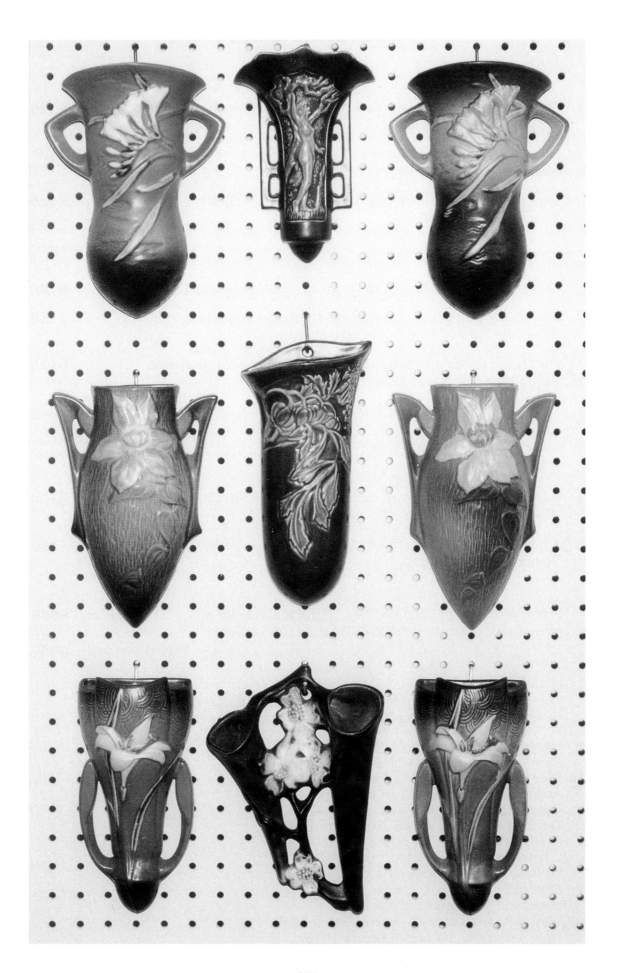

255

Roseville Pottery

ROW 1:

    1. Wincraft pattern, blue, circa 1948, marked in relief   **$125 - 175**
       "*Roseville U.S.A. 267-5*".

    2. Snowberry pattern, blue, circa 1946, marked in relief   **$150 - 200**
       "*Roseville U.S.A. 1WP-8*".

    3. Wincraft pattern, blue circa 1948, marked in relief   **$100 - 150**
       "*Roseville U.S.A. 266-4*".

ROW 2:

    1. Florentine pattern, brown color, circa 1924, unmarked.   **$150 - 200**

    2. Snowberry pattern, dusty rose, 1946, marked in relief   **$150 - 200**
       "*Roseville U.S.A. 1WP-8*".

    3. Florentine pattern with handle, brown, circa 1924, marked   **$125 - 175**
       with a blue ink stamp "*Rv*".

ROW 3:

    1. Foxglove pattern, blue circa 1942, marked in relief "*Roseville* **$200 - 250**
       U.S.A. 1292-8".

    2. Snowberry pattern, green, circa 1946, marked in relief   **$150 - 200**
       "*Roseville U.S.A. 1WP-8*".

    3. Apple Blossom pattern, blue, 1948, marked in relief   **$150 - 200**
       "*Roseville U.S.A. 366-8*".

ROW 4:   A pair of Poppy pattern pockets, with candle holders,   each –**$325 - 375**
         pink, mark impressed "ROSEVILLE", #1281-8" tall.

                                    Priced per pair – **$650 - 750**

NOTE:

The following is a list of Roseville wall pockets (Patterns/colors) that were in our first wall pocket book, but are not in this book.

Page 260: Blackberry pattern, circa 1933.
              Pine Cone pattern, double, brown, circa 1931.
              Clematis pattern, blue color, circa 1944.
              Apple Blossom pattern, green, circa 1948.
              Gardenia pattern, blue, circa late 1940's.
              Gardenia pattern, brown, circa late 1940's.
Page 262: Donatello pattern, 10", circa 1915.
              Carnelian I pattern, blue, circa 1910.
              La Rose pattern, 9", circa 1924.
Page 264: Florentine pattern, 7", circa 1924.
              Imperial I pattern, 8", circa 1916.
Page 266: Wincraft pattern, 8½", brown, circa 1948.
              Ivory I pattern, 10", circa before 1916.
              Mostique pattern, 10½", circa 1915.

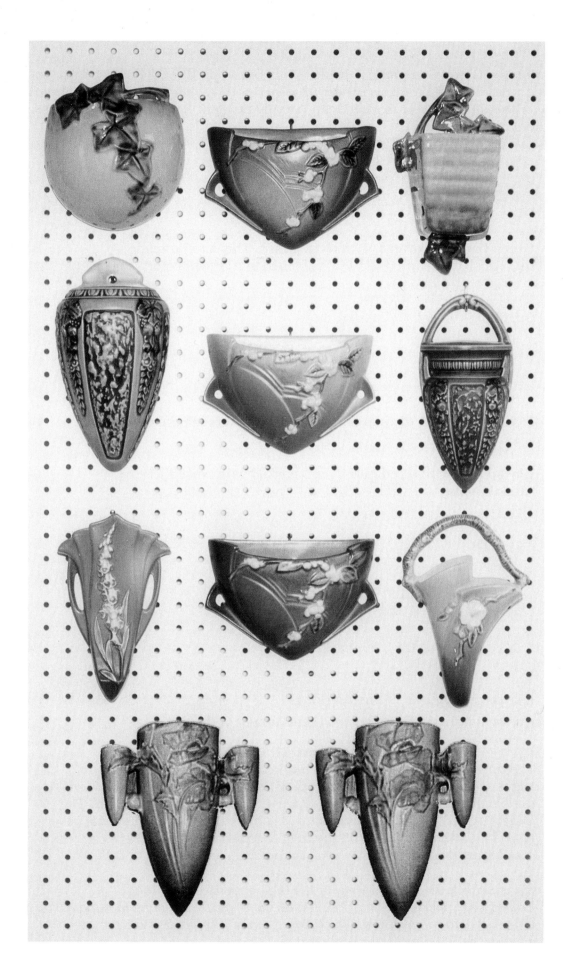

257

ROYAL COPLEY

Spaulding China Company, Sebring, Ohio, began producing Royal Copley pottery in 1942 and continued until 1957. Often confused with other pottery like Shawnee and American Bisque, Royal Copley, although often not marked, can usually be identified by the bright airbrushed colors and the runners on the bottom.

ROW 1:

1. Small blue Angel, 6", no markings.   **$30 - 35**

2. Green bamboo pattern, 7", no markings. This can be made   **$30 - 40**
   into an electric lamp, and it also comes in a brown color.

3. Small pink Angel, 6", no markings.   **$30 - 35**

ROW 2:

1. Pigtail girl in red, 7", marked with raised letters "*Royal Copley*".   **$40 - 45**

2. Gloved lady with a red hat, 6 1/2", marked with raised letters   **$40 - 50**
   "*Royal Copley*".

3. Pigtail girl in aqua, 7", marked with raised letters "*Royal Copley*".   **$40 - 45**

ROW 3:

1. A large blue Angel, 8", no markings.   **$40 - 45**

2. A large pink Angel, 8", no markings.   **$40 - 45**

NOTE:

The angels above were originally marked with paper labels. The only colors we have found them in are pink (red) and blue. The hair colors are blonde and brown, although it seems more blondes are found. The angels can be found as planters as well as wall pockets. The wall pockets are made to hang on the wall or to sit on a shelf. There are also lamps made similar to these, except the wings were left off.

Please check the sizes closely in the descriptions on all Royal Copley wall pockets in this chapter, as some pieces have been super-imposed onto the pictures, which could make it difficult to determine size by the 1" holes in the pegboard.

259

Royal Copley

ROW 1:

1. Farmer boy, green and red, 6$\frac{1}{2}$", marked with raised letters "*Royal Copley*". **$30 - 35**

2. Pirate, grey head band, 8$\frac{1}{2}$", marked with raised letters, "*Royal Copley*", and also it comes with a red head band, (grey is the most difficult to find). **$60 - 65**
   Price with red head band – **$50 - 55**

3. Farmer girl, green and red, 6$\frac{1}{2}$", marked with raised letters "*Royal Copley*". **$30 - 35**

ROW 2:

1. A boy smiling, green clothes with a rare chartreuse hat, 7$\frac{1}{2}$", marked with raised letters "*Royal Copley*". **$40 - 45**

2. Chinese girl smiling, green clothes and a rare chartreuse hat, 7$\frac{1}{2}$", marked with raised letters "© *Royal Copley*". **$40 - 45**

3. A girl with puckered lips, green clothes and a rare chartreuse hat, 7$\frac{1}{2}$", marked with raised letters "*Royal Copley*". **$40 - 45**

ROW 3:

1. Farmer boy, blue and yellow, 6$\frac{1}{2}$", marked with raised letters "*Royal Copley*". **$30 - 35**

2. Chinese girl smiling, red clothes with a grey hat, 7$\frac{1}{2}$", marked with raised letters "*Royal Copley*". **$30 - 35**

3. Farmer girl, blue and yellow, 6$\frac{1}{2}$", marked with raised letters "*Royal Copley*". **$30 - 35**

NOTE:

The above two Chinese girls will always be found with smiling lips. There are also Chinese boys made with puckered lips. All can be found in the following colors.

A. Green clothes with yellow hat.
B. Green clothes with chartreuse hat.
C. Red clothes with grey hat.
D. Red clothes with blue hat.
E. Red clothes with chartreuse hat.

Ones with the blue hats are difficult to find, but the chartreuse hats are very rare.
The boy and girl in ROW 2 can be found in these colors.
A. Green clothes with yellow hat.
B. Green clothes with chartreuse hat.
C. Red clothes with blue hat.

Again, the chartreuse hats are rare.

Royal Copley

ROW 1:

1. Hen, 6⅝", marked with raised letters "*Royal Copley*". **$30 - 35**

2. Tony, 8¾", no markings, (it had a paper label). This piece is called "Tony" because it was designed by Tony Priolo. **$60 - 75**

3. Rooster, 6⅝", marked with raised letters "*Royal Copley*". **$30 - 35**

Priced per pair – **$65 - 75**

ROW 2:

1. Large pink hat with yellow flowers, 6⅞", marked with raised letter "*Royal Copley*". **$30 - 40**

2. Bare shoulder lady, blue hat, 6", marked with raised letters "*Royal Copley*". **$40 - 50**

3. Large yellow hat with pink flowers, 6⅞", marked with raised letters "*Royal Copley*". **$30 - 40**

ROW 3:

1. Small blue hat, 5½", marked with raised letters "*Royal Copley*". **$25 - 35**

2. Bare shoulder lady, red hat, 6", marked with raised letters "*Royal Copley*". **$40 - 50**

3. Small red hat, 5½", marked with raised letters "*Royal Copley*". **$25 - 35**

ROW 4:

1. Princess Blackamoor, grey and yellow, star on necklace, 8", marked with raised letters "*Royal Copley*". **$70 - 85**

2. Gloved lady with blue hat, 6½", marked with raised letters "*Royal Copley*". **$40 - 50**

3. Prince Blackamoor, grey and yellow, plate on necklace, 8", marked with raised letters "*Royal Copley*". **$50 - 60**

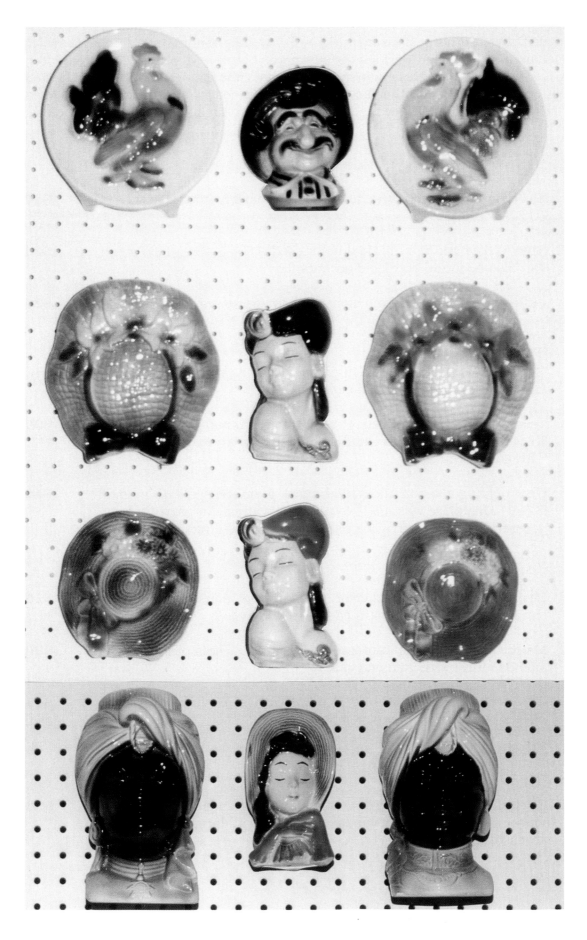

SHAWNEE POTTERY

In 1937 two brothers, Malcolm and Roy Schweiker bought a plant in Zanesville, Ohio that had been used to make tile. They decided the setup was better for making decorated pottery, so they hired Addis E. Hull Jr., a ceramics engineer and at that time general manager of the family owned A.E. Hull Pottery Company and other key people to help design and mold, and began production officially in August of 1937. Shawnee made art pottery and kitchenwares until they closed in 1961.

ROW 1:

    1. Little Bo Peep/Lamb, blue in color, the mark is impressed "U.S.A. 586".   **$30 - 40**

    2. Bow, yellow and red, marked impressed "U.S.A. 434". This piece can also be found with gold accents.   **$25 - 30**

    3. Little Jack Horner, red in color, mark is impressed "U.S.A. 585".   **$30 - 40**

ROW 2:

    1. Grandfather clock, mark is impressed "U.S.A. 1261". This piece can also be found with gold accents.   **$40 - 45**

    2. Telephone, in colors of yellow, red and green, mark is impressed "U.S.A. 529". This piece can also be found in an ivory color with gold accents.   **$30 - 35**

    3. Chef holding a spoon and skillet, mark is impressed with a small "USA". This piece was made to use as a wall pocket or with accessories added, could be used as a wall hanging electric lamp.   **$40 - 50**

ROW 3:

    1. Cornucopia/Bird, blue in color, no markings, some of the birds can be found with cold painted beaks and eyes.   **$15 - 20**

    2. Mantle clock, mark is impressed "U.S.A. 530". This piece can also be found with gold accents.   **$30 - 35**

    3. Cornucopia/Bird, pink colored, no markings. We have seen this piece in blue, pink, green, yellow and ivory.   **$15 - 20**

ROW 4:

    Elf sitting on a log with a spider web in the background, no markings. This can be used as an electric wall lamp with the accessories.   **$50 - 75**

Shawnee Pottery

ROW 1:

    1. Wheat design, no markings, 4 3/4" tall.   **$30 - 35**

☆ 2. Bow, mark impressed "U.S.A. 434", 4" tall.   **$25 - 30**

☆ 3. Star, mark impressed "U.S.A.", 6" tall.   **$40 - 50**

    4. Daffodil design, no markings, 6 3/4" tall.   **$35 - 40**

    5. Red feather design, no markings, 4 3/4" tall.   **$30 - 35**

ROW 2:

☆ 1. Sunflower, mark impressed "U.S.A. 433", 5 1/2".   **$40 - 50**

    2. Sunflower, impressed "U.S.A.", 6 3/4" tall, and has three mold tips on the back like the ones on the cornucopia with a bird.   **$40 - 50**

☆ 3. Elf on log, no markings, 6 1/2" tall. Can be made into a wall hanging electric lamp.   **$50 - 75**

    4. Cornucopia/Bird, no markings, 6" tall. It has three tips on the back like the sunflower.   **$15 - 20**

    5. Cornucopia/Butterfly, no markings, 6" tall. It has three tips on the back like the sunflower.   **$20 - 25**

ROW 3:

☆ 1. Mantle clock, impressed "U.S.A. 530", 6".   **$30 - 35**

☆ 2. Grandfather clock, impressed "U.S.A. 1261", 7" tall.   **$40 - 45**

    3. Granddaughter electric clock, 10" sq. and has two hanging pockets, no markings, 37 1/2" total.   **$75 - 90**

☆ 4. Birds/House, impressed "U.S.A. 830", 5 3/4".   **$30 - 40**

☆ 5. Birds/House, impressed "U.S.A.", 6" tall.   **$25 - 35**

ROW 4:

☆ 1. Girl/Rag Doll, impressed "USA 810", 6 1/4".   **$45 - 55**

    2. Scotty dog, no markings, 9 1/2" tall.   **$50 - 60**

    3. Chef, impressed "U.S.A.", 7 1/2" tall. Can be made into a wall hanging electric lamp.   **$40 - 50**

☆ 4. Telephone, impressed "U.S.A. 529", 6".   **$30 - 35**

ROW 5:

☆ 1. Jack Horner, impressed "U.S.A. 585", 5".   **$30 - 40**

☆ 2. Bo Peep, impressed "U.S.A. 586", 5" tall.   **$30 - 40**

☆ **NOTE:** All will sit or stand as a vase or hang on a wall.

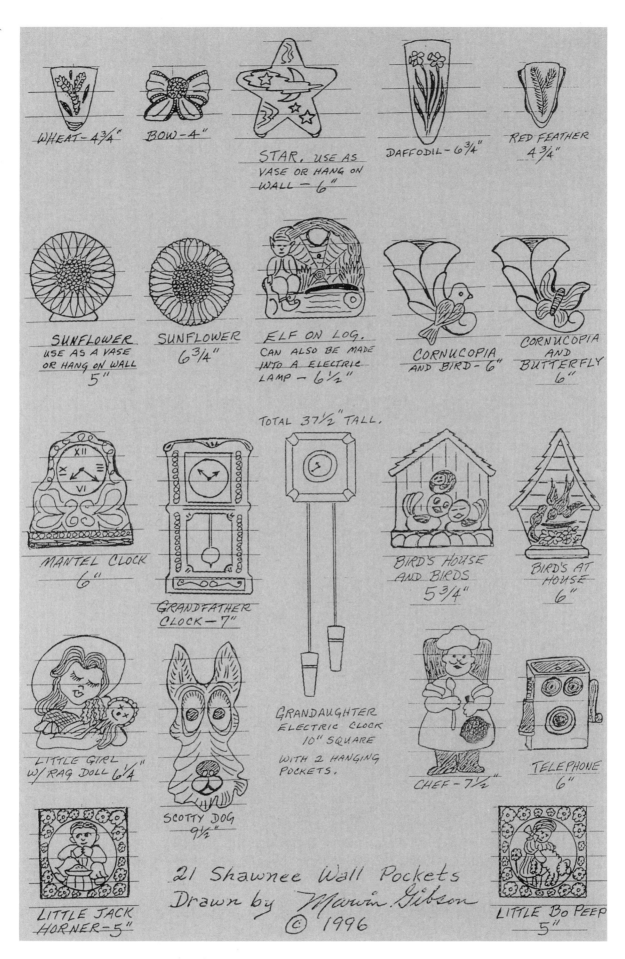

WHEAT—4¾"

BOW—4"

STAR, USE AS
VASE OR HANG ON
WALL — 6"

DAFFODIL—6¾"

RED FEATHER
4¾"

SUNFLOWER
USE AS A VASE
OR HANG ON WALL
5"

SUNFLOWER
6¾"

ELF ON LOG,
CAN ALSO BE MADE
INTO A ELECTRIC
LAMP — 6½"

CORNUCOPIA
AND BIRD — 6"

CORNUCOPIA
AND
BUTTERFLY
6"

TOTAL 37½" TALL.

MANTEL CLOCK
6"

GRANDFATHER
CLOCK — 7"

GRANDAUGHTER
ELECTRIC CLOCK
10" SQUARE
WITH 2 HANGING
POCKETS.

BIRD'S HOUSE
AND BIRDS
5¾"

BIRD'S AT
HOUSE
6"

LITTLE GIRL
W/ RAG DOLL 6¼"

SCOTTY DOG
9½"

CHEF — 7½"

TELEPHONE
6"

LITTLE JACK
HORNER—5"

21 Shawnee Wall Pockets
Drawn by Marvin Gibson
© 1996

LITTLE BO PEEP
5"

267

TAIWAN

Taiwan is an island off the coast of China and is part of the Republic of China. Within the small area of Taiwan, green mountains, lush farmlands, orchards filled with succulent fruits, and fishing vessels lying peacefully at anchor contrast with the broad highways, high-rise buildings and industrial complexes. These and the smiles on the faces of the people are proof of peace and prosperity that exist in Taiwan. The wall pockets we see today that come from Taiwan are not made of the high quality materials that we have become accustomed to, but are mass produced for the competitive market.

ROW 1:

1. Santa head, white trimmed with Christmas colors, marked with a paper label "MADE IN TAIWAN ITEM #T17273".   **$15 - 20**

2. Ladies head, white, pink and grey, marked with a gold colored foil label "MADE IN TAIWAN".   **$15 - 20**

ROW 2:

1. Girls face with art deco design, white, pink and blue, marked with gold colored foil label "MADE IN TAIWAN".   **$15 - 20**

2. White fan, marked with a gold colored foil label "MADE IN TAIWAN".   **$10 - 15**

ROW 3:

1. Folded pocket, white and pink with floral design, marked with a gold colored foil label "MADE IN TAIWAN".   **$10 - 15**

2. Little lamb's head with blue eyes, marked with a gold colored foil label "MADE IN TAIWAN".   **$15 - 20**

NOTE:
Although the wall pockets from Taiwan do not have the quality of the older wall pockets, they do have a certain charm of their own. For those of us who like a modern look they can be a nice addition to our decor.

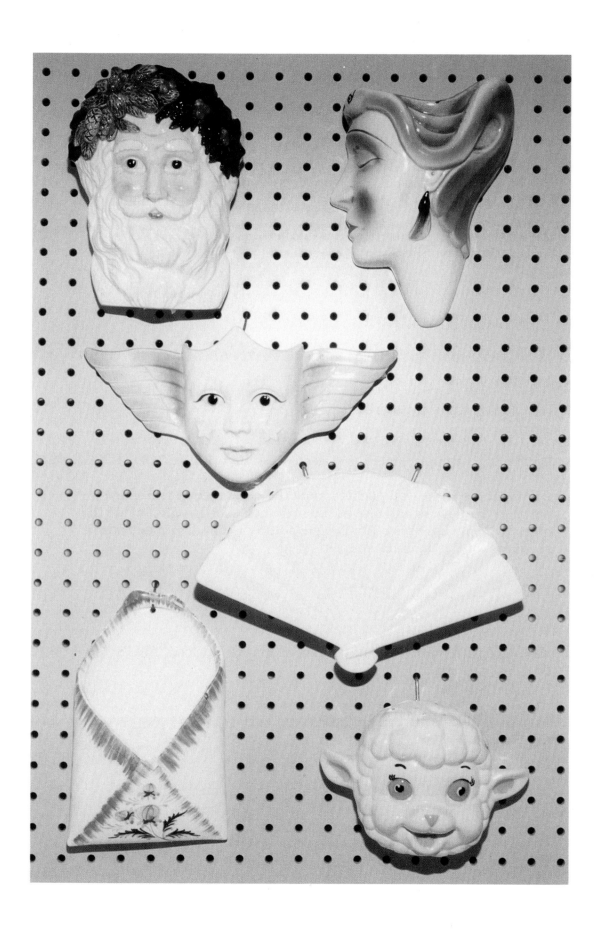

VAN BRIGGLE POTTERY

Van Briggle Pottery began in Colorado Springs, Colorado in 1901 by Artus Van Briggle and his wife Anne. Artus died in 1904, but Anne continued with the pottery and it is still in operation today. The public can tour the pottery and buy pieces in the showrooms. There is also a Van Briggle Museum in Colorado Springs.

ROW 1:

    1. Parrot, mulberry, mark is incised "30 AA Van Briggle Colo Spgs".   **$225 - 275**

    2. Vase type, turquoise, art deco design, mark is incised "AA VAN BRIGGLE COLO, SPGS".   **$175 - 225**

ROW 2:

    1. Double lily, turquoise, mark is incised "AA VAN BRIGGLE Colo. Spgs".   **$175 - 225**

    2. Double lily, mulberry, mark is incised "AA VAN BRIGGLE Colo. Spgs".   **$175 - 225**

    3. Double lily, turquoise, mark is incised "3 AA Van Briggle COLO SPGS".   **$175 - 225**

    On the above three wall pockets, note the difference in the space between the flowers and also #1 has two holes for hanging while the other two only have one. Van Briggle pottery is hand trimmed which accounts for the different shapes.

ROW 3:

    1. Vase type with flower design, turquoise, mark is incised "AA 18 Van Briggle Colo. Spgs".   **$200 - 250**

    2. Vase type with flower design, mulberry, mark is incised "AA 14 Van Briggle COLO. SPGS".   **$200 - 250**

    The above two wall pockets had a catalog #852, made from 1922-1926.

271

WELLER POTTERY

The Weller Pottery was founded by Mr. Sam Weller at Fultonham, Ohio in 1873 and became a legend in the pottery field over the next 75 years. The pottery was moved to Zanesville, Ohio in 1882 and in 1893 began making art pottery. The Weller Pottery had some very famous artists designing and decorating art ware for them. Artists like Frank Ferrell, Fredrick Rhead and Jacques Sicardo among others, helped make Weller Pottery one of the best known potteries in the United States. Weller Pottery closed in 1948.

ROW 1:

1. Blossom pattern, green with red blossoms, circa late 1930's, mark is impressed "WELLER".   **$100 - 125**

2. Floral pattern, pink with multicolored flowers, circa late 1930's, mark is impressed "WELLER".   **$100 - 125**

ROW 2:

Sydonia pattern, double pockets, blue color, circa 1920's, marked with a black and white paper label, "*Wellers Pottery*".   **$125 - 150**

ROW 3:

1. Orris Ware Pattern, ivory and brown, circa 1914, no markings.   **$100 - 125**

2. Marvo pattern, brown on brown color, circa mid 1920's, no markings.   **$100 - 125**

NOTE:
We have found that the production period makes very little difference in a wall pocket's price. What matters most is the design and color. Applied figures or the unusual shape like the double pocket above seem to bring premium prices . Weller wall pockets can still be found at a reasonable price and are certainly worth the investment.

Weller Pottery

1. Lido pattern, blue color, circa late 1930's, no markings.   **$125 - 150**

2. Oak leaf pattern, brown color, circa pre-1936, mark is
    incised "*Weller*".   **$125 - 150**

ROW 2:

Blue drapery pattern, blue with red flowers, circa 1915-1920,   **$150 - 175**
mark is impressed "WELLER".

ROW 3:

1. Roma pattern, ivory with red flowers, circa 1914, no markings.   **$125 - 150**

2. Klyro pattern, grey and blue with red blossoms and blue berries,   **$100 - 125**
    circa late 1920's, no markings.

NOTE:

*Samuel A. Weller started his pottery in a small way on his farm, using
the clay from his own land making utility wares for his own use.
He then went on to selling his wares, most likely door to door in
Zanesville, Ohio. Although Weller Pottery was one of the first of the
well known potteries to go into business in Zanesville, Ohio, it is not as
popular today as some of the other potteries of that era. That does not
make it any less attractive to the collectors who collect it with a
passion. The quality of Weller wall pockets are second to none.
Samuel Weller had some of the best known artists in the country
working for him over the years. Although Weller made many wall
pockets, after nine years of collecting we have only twenty three in
our own collection.*

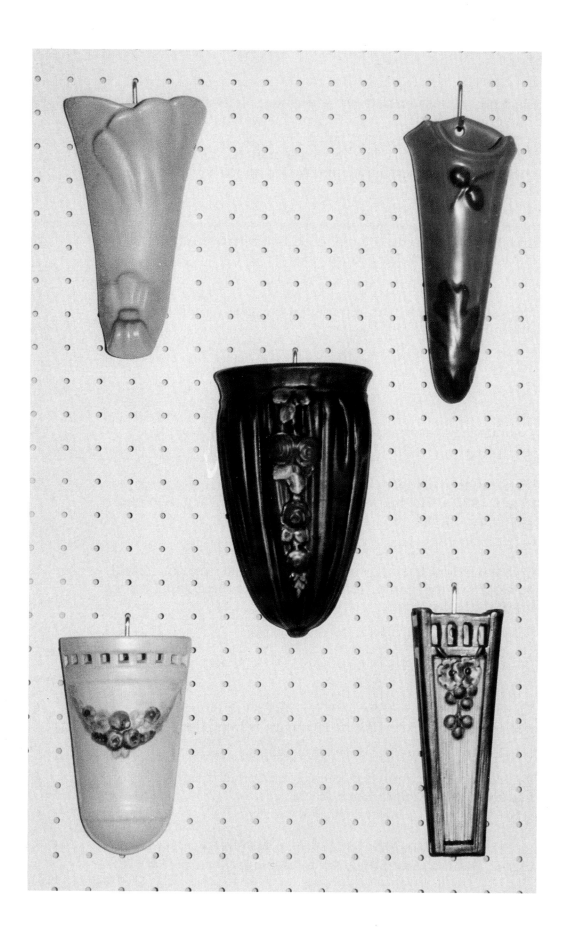

275

Weller Pottery

ROW 1:

1. Blackberry/blossom pattern, aqua blue, no markings and (could not verify the pattern). A picture of this wall pocket was sent to several collectors, but none could positively identify it. The Weller "Gloria" pattern is a very close match. The color, glaze, shape and feel is very much like Weller, so we have included it in this chapter.   **$75 - 100**

2. Arcadia pattern, pink colored, circa mid to late 1930's. The mark is incised "*Weller Pottery since 1872 A-5*".   **$75 - 100**

3. Floral pattern, blue with red iris flower, mark is impressed "WELLER".   **$75 - 100**

ROW 2:

1. Colonial lady pattern, aqua blue, no markings.   **$125 - 150**

2. Roma pattern, (Dupont design) ivory color, circa late teens to late 1920's. The mark is impressed "WELLER", it also has a blue ink stamp "15".   **$125 - 150**

3. Colonial lady pattern, lavender color, no Weller markings, but has a brown ink stamp "12X", and also has the original selling price of $1.25 on back.   **$125 - 150**

ROW 3:

1. Roma pattern, ivory color with red roses and blue berries, circa late teens – late 1920's. The mark is impressed "WELLER".   **$100 - 125**

2. Panella pattern, tan to brown color, circa mid to late 1930's, marked "*Weller Pottery Since 1872*".   **$100 - 125**

3. Floral pattern, blue color with multicolored flowers, no Weller marks, but written on the back in blue ink "*Shower Gift 1927*".   **$100 - 125**

Weller Pottery

ROW 1:

    1. Klyro pattern, grey and blue with red blossoms and blue berries, circa late 1920's, no markings. This piece is wider at the top than the one shown earlier in this chapter.   **$75 - 100**

    2. Klyro pattern, round style, grey and blue with red blossoms and blue berries, circa late 1920's. The mark is impressed "WELLER".   **$125 - 150**

    3. Woodrose pattern, blue color, circa before 1920, no markings.   **$75 - 90**

ROW 2:

    1. Woodrose pattern, brown color, circa before 1920, no Weller marks, but it does have an "8" incised on the back side.   **$75 - 100**

    2. Woodrose pattern, lavender color, circa before 1920, no markings.   **$75 - 100**

    3. Woodrose pattern, aqua blue color, circa before 1920, no Weller marks, but it has an "8" incised on the back.   **$75 - 100**

ROW 3:

    1. Woodrose pattern, small size, brown color, circa before 1920, no markings.   **$60 - 90**

    2. Woodrose pattern, medium size, brown color, circa before 1920. The mark is impressed "WELLER".   **$75 - 100**

    This piece is also made in a large size. We have also seen one in the brown color that we thought was a Weller, but when we picked it up, it was very lightweight and impressed "MADE IN JAPAN". This is another example of the way Japan copied other countries wares.

    3. Tutone pattern, maroon with green leaves and berries, circa late 1920's, no markings, 10 1/2" tall. This piece was priced by a dealer and sold by him for $235.00.   **$225 - 250**

Weller Pottery

ROW 1:

    1. Roba pattern, green and white color with yellow blossoms, circa mid-late 1930's, mark is incised *"Weller Pottery since 1872"*.   **$125 - 150**

    2. Pink and white color with blue blossoms. <u>THIS IS NOT WELLER</u>. Made of chalk, but looks like the "Weller Roba Pattern", no markings.   **$20 - 25**

ROW 2:

    1. Woodcraft pattern, small limb with pink blossoms, circa early 1920's until early 1930's, no markings.   **$110 - 135**

    2. Woodcraft pattern, small limb with red blossoms, circa early 1920's until the early 1930's, no markings.   **$110 - 135**

    3. Yellow and green color. <u>THIS IS NOT WELLER</u>. This is to show how a company can make a replica (copy cat) reproduction of an original design. This is a copy of the Weller Woodcraft pattern, small limb with blossoms. This yellow and green piece is marked incised "DADSON CALIF. 9".   **$25 - 30**

ROW 3:

    1. Woodcraft pattern, large limb with leaves and fruit, circa early 1920's until early 1930's, mark is impressed "WELLER".   **$150 - 200**

    2. Woodcraft pattern, squirrel on tree trunk, circa early 1920's until the early 1930's, no Weller markings, but it has a brown ink stamped "25".   **$300 - 350**

NOTE:

The wall pockets on this page that are not Weller were put here to show how easy it is to be mistaken about the identity of some wall pockets. Be sure to check each piece very carefully and get to know the patterns, marks, colors and glazes of the potteries you collect. As we have shown in this book, there was a lot of copying going on among the hundreds of potteries in this country and other countries as well.

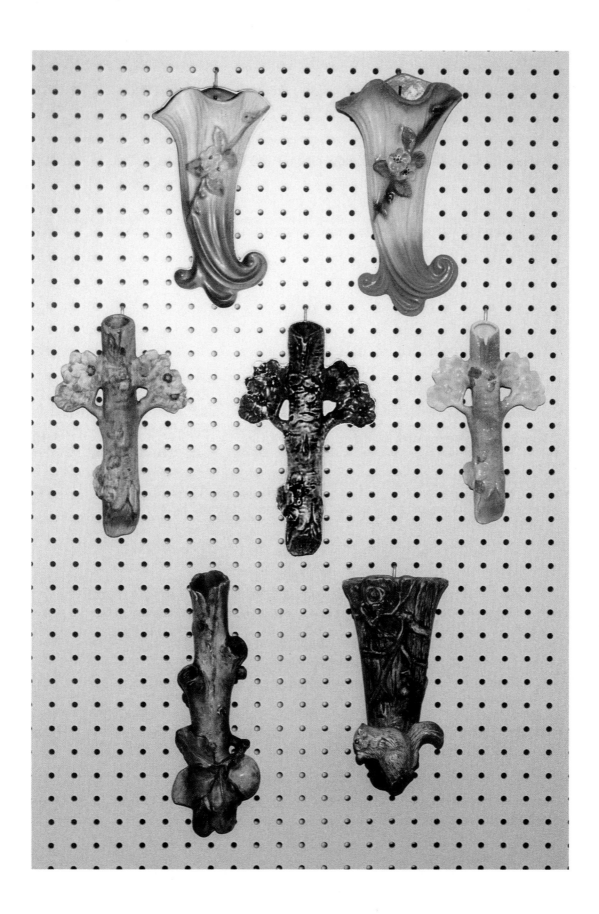

Weller Pottery

ROW 1:

    1. Woodrose pattern, medium size, aqua color, circa before 1920, mark is impressed "WELLER", 7" tall.   **$75 - 95**

    2. Teapot (novelty line), white color, circa 1930's, no markings, 9" tall.   **$90 - 100**

    3. Trellis design with pot, aqua color, circa unknown, no markings, 10 1/4" tall.   **$225 - 295**

ROW 2:

    1. Woodcraft pattern, owl in a tree trunk, circa early 1920's until early 1930's. The mark is impressed "WELLER", it also has a brown ink stamp "XX".   **$300 - 350**

    2. Woodcraft pattern, owl in a tree, no markings.   **$300 - 350**

    3. Woodcraft pattern, owl in a tree, mark is impressed "WELLER", and it also has an original paper price label marked "8/20/30 – $2.98".   **$300 - 350**

NOTE:

The three owl wall pockets above are all 10 1/2" tall. Notice the detail on each of the owls–the first one has a smooth finish with very little detail, #2 has a little more detail and the last one has very heavy detail. I think these three wall pockets show the personal touch that each individual artist gave their pieces.

ROW 3:

    1. Ardsley pattern, double pocket, green color with cattail design, circa 1920's, no markings, 12" tall.   **$200 - 250**

    2. Roma pattern (Dupont design), ivory color, circa late teen's-late 1920's, the mark is impressed "WELLER", 8" tall.   **$100 - 150**

    3. Glendale pattern, bird at nest, circa 1920's, mark is impressed "WELLER", 12 1/2" tall.   **$350 - 475**

283

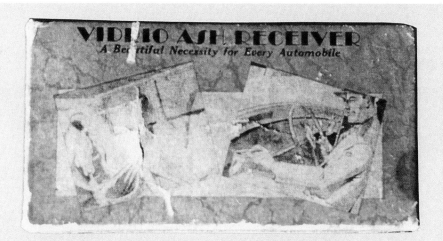

VIDRIO ASH RECEIVER
A Beautiful Necessity for Every Automobile

DIRECTIONS

MODEL A1—A model to fit any width auto door or window sill.
MODEL A2—A model to fit under any bolt on body on dash board.
MODEL A3—A bracket model to fit any dash board.

MFD. BY
VIDRIO PRODUCTS CORP.
Cicero, Ill.

Special Features that make Vidrio Ash Receivers the most popular on the market.

A product that can be installed by anyone. Requiring no drilling or tapping and has an ash receptacle deep enough to keep ashes from blowing out. Holder is beautifully plated and adds a wonderful appearance to any car. Receiver can be instantly emptied and will never discolor or wear out.

VIDRIO
UNIVERSAL
ASH RECEIVER
MODEL No. A

```
* VIDRIO ASH RECEIVER *
View of top, both sides and one end of original
box, also the ash receiver made of multi-colored
glass. This piece glows florescent under a black
light because of uranium used in the glass. This
product was manufactured in the late 1920's until
early 1930's.        1997 price - $50.00 - $60.00
```

Bring the fragrance of flowers *into the* home

Now, let the delicate fragrance of beautiful flowers steal through *your* home—through the hallways and corridors, in the living room, through the bed-chambers, through the bath-rooms. Sanozone Air Perfumes, now so much in vogue, are released subtly by means of artistic and colorful Sanozone Wall Brackets —classic in design.

Replace household odors,—mustiness, stale tobacco smoke, foods etc. —with the exquisite aroma of crushed flowers, a *lasting* fragrance because Sanozone Air Perfumes are made by a secret process from essential oils...Sold by drug and department stores.

Write today for free descriptive circular.

DEALERS: Additional dealers wanted, drug, department stores, phonograph, electrical appliance stores. Write today.

SANOZONE CHEMICAL CO.
1129 Roy Street   Philadelphia

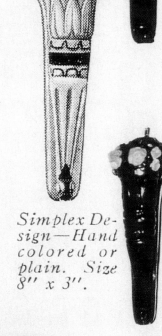

Simplex Design—Hand colored or plain. Size 8″ x 3″.

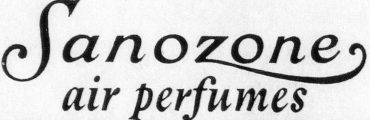

Sanozone
air perfumes